The Home Decorator's
STAMPING BOOK

The Home Decorator's
STAMPING BOOK

LINDA BARKER

Photography by Lizzie Orme

Pastimes™

An Imprint of Martingale & Company

For Chris and Jessica

Text and designs copyright © Eddison Sadd Editions 1997
Photographs copyright © Lizzie Orme 1997 (except page 7)
This edition copyright © Eddison Sadd Editions 1997

Library of Congress Cataloging-in-Publication Data

Barker, Linda.
    The home decorator's stamping book / Linda Barker.
        p.   cm.
    Includes bibliographical references and index.
    ISBN 1–56477–191–1
    1. Rubber stamp printing. 2. Interior decoration. I. Title.
TT867.B37   1998
747' .3—dc21   97–46892
                                                                   CIP

Printed in China
03 02 01 00 99 98 6 5 4 3 2 1

First published in Great Britain in 1997
by Little, Brown and Company (UK)

AN EDDISON•SADD EDITION
Edited, designed and produced by
Eddison Sadd Editions Limited
St Chad's House
148 King's Cross Road
London WC1X9DH
Great Britain

Martingale & Company
PO Box 118
Bothell, WA 98041-0118
www.patchwork.com
by arrangement with
Eddison Sadd Editions Limited

CONTENTS

INTRODUCTION

Linda

All of us want to make our living spaces attractive – it's one of the things that makes home decorating such a challenge: Should you color-wash the walls or rag-roll them? Is the kitchen large enough to accommodate that charming old hutch you've always wanted? There are endless ways to furnish and decorate your home and there are many inspiring photographs in books and magazines from which you can take ideas. When you're starting to think about decorating a room in your home, first gather together all those imaginative books, pictures, and magazine clippings and spread them out on the floor in front of you (preferably in the room you want to decorate) and then try to determine just what it is about those images that you like so much. Notice the colors, styles, and textures and imagine how they would look in your own room. Assess various decorative paint effects and weigh them against the effect that a plain, flat color has on a room. If you like the stamping effect in the Living Room chapter of this book *(see pages 60–65)* but you prefer the palette used in the Bedroom chapter *(see pages 74–79)*, you can simply use whichever color scheme you prefer. Why not use the duck egg blue shade shown on the dressing table in the bedroom to color the walls and then stamp them, using the blocks shown on the wall of the living room? The choice is yours.

Stamping can be great fun and the results are unbelievably quick – you could complete a room within a day or a piece of furniture in a matter of hours. Although the craft of stamping is a relatively new one, it can soon become rather addictive. It's quite by surprise that I find myself to be an avid stamping enthusiast, but show me a plain surface and I will, without a doubt, stamp on it! Apart from those very early attempts at stamping during formative kindergarten years, using lumps of potato and messy paint powders, I'd never really given much thought to stamping – until I spotted one of those tiny wooden printing blocks in my local art supply store. With a quick press of the printing block onto an ink pad, the design was then stamped on a surface – it couldn't have been much easier! Then I began contemplating the many stamped effects possible on furniture and fabrics. The relatively high price of that one tiny block eliminated any desire I might have had to buy a whole armful of blocks, but it also inspired me to learn how to make my own blocks. As a result of my experimentation, I've made many stamping blocks for a fraction of the cost of purchased ones. In this book you'll find complete instructions for making your own blocks, using the stamp designs featured at the back of this book *(see pages 118–125)* or your own unique ideas.

THE ORIGINS OF DECORATIVE PAPERS AND HAND BLOCKING

Long before the advent of wallpaper or decorative painting, all of the bare walls in palaces, castles, villas, and large houses belonging to wealthy Europeans were covered with tapestries or, occasionally, painted cloth. Wood paneling and leather work were also sometimes used for decorating. However, with the introduction of papermaking in the late fifteenth century, a less expensive form of decoration was created – wallpaper. The earliest wallpapers were either hand-painted or stenciled. Later on, decorative techniques evolved in the seventeenth century that led to block printing, which facilitated the production of greater quantities of paper in much less time than ever before.

New, extravagant wallpapers emulated luxurious tapestries and silk wall hangings, using both block printing and also a flocking technique. Fashionable flocked papers were made by dusting powdered fibers over a slow-drying adhesive that was applied to the paper, and these were unequivocally *de rigueur* in the seventeenth century. At the same time, the Chinese produced a range of fine, decorative papers by using etched plates or woodblocks. The color was applied either by stencil or by hand, and many of these papers have survived to this day. Images of printed panoramic scenes and country landscapes, architectural columns, and capitals all appeared in France toward the end of the eighteenth century. These wall coverings were so intricate and precise in style that they required a specialist to hang them.

At first, early wallpapers were quite expensive but, by the beginning of the nineteenth century, the walls in an average room could be papered for a price that was the equivalent of a day's wage, which made papering much cheaper than painting. People then began to use paper for decorating in greater quantities, not only to provide a visual richness, but also to reduce the dampness and drafts that came through their walls. Many inexpensive papers were produced during this era but, unfortunately, the less expensive paper decayed over time, and so it began to lose its wide popularity.

It wasn't until recently that walls painted a solid color were a common sight, due to the high cost of the work and because paint stained easily. The relatively new do-it-yourself movement has really changed the face of home decorating. New paints and easy-to-use products help eliminate the usual drudgery of home decorating and never before has it been so accessible to so many.

When I began, I was eager to learn how a stamp could be used to decorate large areas, such as all of the wall surfaces in a room. My first attempts at stamping were very encouraging and my conclusion was, of course, that stamps are a brilliant way of creating an all-over effect and, in addition, are much simpler to use than stencils, which require careful alignment. For applying an all-over

The block store at Arthur Sanderson & Sons (top), *where sets of wooden blocks for 340 different designs are carefully stacked. These include the Acanthus design* (below) *created by William Morris in 1875, which is still available today.*

pattern, stenciling requires more of an artistic skill, whereas stamping is far more immediate and, therefore, much easier to control.

For many years stenciling has been used to emulate the effects of exquisite but expensive wallpapers, particularly when the papers were first produced by highly skilled craftsmen. The technique of stamping can also be used to re-create these same effects with great success. Historically, the printing process used to create those wonderful old hand-blocked papers was, in fact, achieved with huge wooden printing blocks that were lowered onto plain paper fitted onto enormous printing presses. At first the block was loaded with the color and then lowered carefully over the roll of paper, using the registration marks for precise alignment. Each color needed a separate printing block, and more intricate papers required several blocks in order to make up their pattern. As you can imagine, the cost was prohibitive for most home owners, but the stunning beauty and intricate craftsmanship that went into these papers were inevitably reflected in the cost. Some of the original blocks are still in existence today, and these are still used by producers of fine wallpapers, although you can expect to pay a princely sum for them. The exceptional quality of hand-blocked paper doesn't come cheap: cost is directly related to the quality of materials, richness of colors, and the amount of time it takes a skilled worker to produce such a glorious product. Today in a similar but far humbler way, we're trying to capture the unique effect of this hand-blocked quality with our own printing blocks.

USING STAMPS TO ACHIEVE A HAND-BLOCKED EFFECT

You will soon discover that quite detailed motifs can be cut from soft foam rubber to produce intricate shapes and patterns. Stamping produces a somewhat cruder, but no less effective, imitation of hand blocking, which can (rather more affordably) be re-created in our own homes to achieve, if not the same quality as that of old, hand-blocked paper, something that is, without a doubt, far more attractive and affordable than some of the mass-produced modern wallpapers sold in decorating stores.

Like the hand-blocking technique that was used so many years ago, a good stamping effect requires careful registration of the block to line up the pattern of the design, and a strong, even pressure must be applied to the back of the block to transfer the paint evenly. With the technique of stamping, you can not necessarily re-create those wonderful old wallpaper designs, but you can certainly use them as inspiration for making an interesting design that creates a bold impact in your home with a small impact on your budget.

An interesting effect that appears on the surface of stamped designs, characteristic of the hand-blocking technique, is the slightly dimpled surface of the paint, which occurs when a block is lifted away from the surface upon which the block has been set. The effect is a result of the paint being lifted ever so slightly as the block is pulled away from the flat surface. Dimpling sometimes occurs on hand-blocked papers too and is a particularly charming characteristic of a stamped motif, whether it appears on an expensive paper or on your own hand-stamped designs.

In this book, I'll show you how to design your own image for a stamping block (for when you're feeling creative), but you could also choose simply to use one of the patterns provided at the back of this book *(see pages 118–125)*. As is often the case, some of the simplest designs can look just as stunning as the more elaborate and more complex designs. Even a simply drawn heart or star motif can be quickly sketched (even by those who consider themselves to be artistically challenged) to produce some great results.

MAKING YOUR OWN STAMPING BLOCK

Once you've decided on a motif, trace the design onto a piece of white paper and decide whether it needs to be enlarged or reduced on a photocopier. You may find it easier to start with a small stamp design at first because, when printing, a small block is simpler to control than a large one, particularly when you're working on vertical surfaces or large pieces of furniture. Once your design is the right size, cut away the excess white paper. Use a small amount of spray mount, in a well-ventilated room, to provide a 'just-tacky' surface for holding the paper template on a piece of foam rubber. If you apply too much spray, you'll find it difficult to peel away the paper from the foam rubber after the rubber shape has been cut. You'll also find that too little spray will not hold the sheet in place. Spray mount can be expensive so, instead of purchasing a can for this purpose alone, you could just as easily hold the template in place with ordinary dressmaker's pins pushed through the paper into the foam rubber. Use a small pair of scissors or a sharp craft knife to cut around the design (I usually use a craft knife because the blades are inexpensive and easily replaced). You'll find that the foam cuts away easily, but take care when cutting around smaller, intricate parts of your designs. Make sure the blade is at a right angle to the surface so you don't undercut the design, and hold the blade at a right angle to the foam.

The size of your block is determined by the size of the image you decide to use. Once you've traced your design and enlarged or reduced it to size, use a ruler to measure both the length and width of the image accurately – remember it will be either square or rectangular. The image should fit neatly inside the block, with the edges of the design just touching the sides of the block. You'll find that the more square the cut of your piece of wood, the easier it will be to correctly align and print the stamped design. Use a carpenter's square (if you have one) to mark off a perfect square and score the lines with a dark pencil before sawing. If your tool kit doesn't include anything that even remotely resembles a carpenter's square, you can line up your measurements with the corner of a piece of paper or a book, or you could even use a CD case – anything that has perfect right angles.

I often use MDF (medium-density fiberboard) for making blocks because it is strong, easy to cut, and does not warp. (Always wear a protective face mask when sawing MDF; its tiny dust particles should not be inhaled – and the dust will float everywhere, especially if you're using a jigsaw.) However, almost any material could be used for a block, provided it's easy to saw and thick enough to hold between your fingertips at the sides. In my own eagerness to get started, I've cut pieces of old paneling for my blocks when a trip to the lumberyard seemed just too far, and this has worked out perfectly well! For the tiny black stamps that were printed on the tiled splashback featured in the Bathroom chapter *(see pages 92–95)*, I used one of the tiny mosaic tiles to make the actual block. However, this particular project was an exception and, when sawing wood to make the blocks, you must first carefully align the cutting edge of the saw with the marked lines. Cut the wood and smooth down any rough edges using sandpaper to create a perfect block that's ready for the foam rubber to be applied.

Make sure that you trace your design onto both large surfaces of the block; you will soon discover that the outline on one side of the block is critical for correct alignment of the pieces of foam rubber. The outline that you've traced onto what will be the top of the block will help you to position it correctly when stamping on a surface, because you won't be able to see the underside of the block. Use contact cement to adhere the foam rubber pieces to the block, ensuring a perfect bond; when it's dry you'll be ready to begin stamping. Detailed step-by-step photographs and additional instructions on the technique of making a stamp can be found later on in the Getting Started section *(see pages 32–33)*.

I hope you will enjoy making the projects I've designed especially for this book and that you may feel inspired to start creating your own design motifs. Put your own stamp upon your home!

Part One

TECHNIQUES

This section of the book outlines all the techniques that you'll need to get started on your stamping projects. It provides detailed step-by-step instructions for the paint finishes most commonly recommended for use in conjunction with stamped designs. In these pages you'll also find out how to make your own stamping block and, more important, how to apply it on various surfaces as well as how to embellish your stamped design once it's printed.

You'll also find advice on buying paints, choosing colors, and deciding which surfaces to stamp on — everything you could possibly need to get started.

MATERIALS AND EQUIPMENT

All the materials and equipment that you really need to start stamping are very basic items, such as wood scraps, adhesives, and latex paints, that are generally found in most homes. Foam rubber is readily available in art, hobby, and crafts stores as well as in many home-improvement outlets. You'll also find foam suppliers listed in your local phone directory, and some may even have a mail-order service. Foam is generally sold by the yard or meter in ⅛-in (3-mm) sheets. Everything else should be easy to find and, unlike with many other crafts, you don't need to spend a lot of money to begin. In fact, long before the more sophisticated woodblock came into its own, there was the humble potato print, and some of the less complicated motifs, such as stars or hearts, can still be printed with a potato. You can try stamping first with a potato. Once you've become proficient, you can move on to stamps made of foam and wood.

STAMPING BLOCK

Fundamental to beginning, small scraps of MDF (medium-density fiberboard) or wood are used to make the stamping block. Often a home-improvement store or lumber-yard will have a stack of scraps of this type of material so you may not have to pay much, if anything, for it. Some stores will give you scraps for free – it really depends on the amount of wood that you need for your project. Make sure that the scrap is a good thickness, ideally 1 in (25 mm) or more, which will enable you to hold the stamp easily along the sides of the block. Some home-improvement stores offer a cutting service that is available for a small charge, but you may find that they can't cut small blocks.

FOAM RUBBER

Available in sheets, foam rubber can be purchased in stores in a variety of thicknesses. It's generally black or white in color. For stamping purposes, thicknesses of ⅛, ¹¹⁄₆₄, or ¹³⁄₆₄ in (approximately 3, 4, or 5 mm) are ideal.

SAWS, SANDPAPERS, AND STEEL WOOL

The wood or MDF that's used for the stamping block can be easily cut using a small tenon saw or a jigsaw, if you have one. (Always wear a protective face mask when cutting MDF.) Mark the cutting lines clearly with a pencil, using a carpenter's square or T-square to ensure that the block is cut precisely. Once the block is cut, you'll need to smooth the rough edges. There are many different grades of sandpaper available on the market and they'll all do a good job. There's no need to buy a special type just for stamping; you can use whatever is at hand: rough, coarse, or fine-grade – they'll all give the same desired effect, which is to prevent splinters from getting into your hands! Steel wool is an extremely useful material that is available in a number of different grades (as is sandpaper), ranging from coarse to medium to fine. It's often used to distress colors to achieve an antiqued and distressed-paint effect, and it can also be used to apply beeswax whenever this type of finish is desired.

CRAFT KNIVES

You'll need a very sharp blade (and a cutting mat) to cut cleanly through foam rubber. A craft knife is the best tool for the job, and it can be purchased at art or crafts stores. If you don't have a craft knife, a utility knife is perfectly acceptable but, for the cleanest cuts, always use a new blade. Be sure to replace the blade frequently, whenever it starts to pull or drag on the foam sheet. Alternatively, small, sharp scissors can also be used for cutting foam, but sharp cutting edges are essential; dull blades can cause accidents and will yield poor results.

ADHESIVE

For stamping, contact cement is the only adhesive to use; no other product should be substituted. It provides the strongest bond and enables the stamp to be easily cleaned in water after use. Contact adhesive is applied to both surfaces that are to be bonded together; that is, the back of the foam rubber stamp and the underside of the block. Only when the two glued surfaces are totally dry are the pieces then pressed together to create a strong bond. Press the surfaces gently together, make sure all the foam has made contact with the block, and then it's ready for use.

PAINTS

The kind of paint that you use depends on the type of surface that you're decorating. In general, most of the stamped surfaces in this book use tinted, water-based latex paint. A basic brilliant white paint can be colored using tubes of acrylic to achieve the desired shade. This is the most economical way of creating the perfect color.

Be methodical in your approach to tinting paint. Store everything after use: you'll find that glass jars are ideal for mixing and keeping paint so that you can create and store an entire range of colors. Brushes and other items used with water-based paint can be cleaned with water.

Universal pigments (in several colors) may also be used for tinting paints and varnishes. Use an old paintbrush to mix pigments.

OTHER NEEDS

An ordinary piece of window glass, although not critical to stamping by any stretch of the imagination, is well worth obtaining. It's perfect for holding a thin layer of paint into which you can press your stamp directly for even coverage. Old, chipped dinner plates are also extremely useful for this purpose, but if you're using a large stamp, then these larger blocks will not fit inside the curved rim of an ordinary plate. Always use masking tape to cover the sides of the glass.

A can of spray mount is also very useful. It's used to lightly dust the back of a paper pattern, which is then adhered to the foam rubber. The adhesive holds the pattern in place as a guide for cutting the foam. (Always spray in a well-ventilated room; the glue particles tend to float around and could be harmful if inhaled. Whether you're using spray mount inside or outside, secure sheets of paper around all three sides of the work when you spray to contain the adhesive.

A brayer (hard roller) can be used to even out the paint on a glass surface; it can also be used to transfer paint directly onto the block.

OTHER PAINTS

I occasionally use artist's acrylics on some stamping projects, either for embellishing a stamp with a hand-finished detail, such as the dressing table *(see pages 76–79)*, or for adding details, such as the fine lining on the country-style wall unit *(see pages 112–115)*. The items designed for the nursery are good examples of projects for which I would always choose to use artist's acrylics, principally because they only need a small amount of paint.

Artist's acrylics are available in all well-stocked art supply stores and crafts shops. They come in a wide range of colors, and you can mix and blend two or more colors, if desired, to obtain even more shades.

Both artist's acrylic and gouache (opaque watercolors) are suitable for use when tinting is desired. The acrylic type has a thicker, more slippery quality, and it's the type of color I use most frequently on my decorating projects.

Glass and ceramic paints are special types of paint that should only be used on appropriate surfaces to achieve the best bond between paint and surface. They may have different solvents, such as paint thinner or denatured alcohol. Always check which is the right solvent for your paint, according to the manufacturer's instructions on the label.

DIFFERENT VARNISHES

Polyurethane varnish is oil based and available in several forms. Varnish comes in cans for brushing, and it's also available in spray form. Brushing is more time-consuming

and you need to clean up paintbrushes and solvents afterward. Spraying is quick and easy, but it can be expensive, particularly when working on larger projects.

Brush-on varnish is available in many different colors (mostly wood tones), but it can be tinted to any color using artist's oil colors or universal pigments.

OTHER VARNISHES

Other varnishes can include crackle varnish, which is actually a two-part system. Different varnishes have different drying times and when applied one over the other, they result in a crinkled surface, similar to the effect that you often see on many old paintings. Two-part varnish is available as a two-part water-based varnish, which gives even results every time, and there's a slightly more temperamental oil- and water-based varnish system, which is the most widely available. Make sure you always follow the manufacturer's instructions.

WATER-BASED VERSUS OIL PAINTS

Whenever possible I try to use water-based paints. They are kinder to the environment than oil-based paints, and it's quicker and easier to wash equipment and tools in warm, soapy water. If your piece of furniture is properly prepared, water-based paint has enough adhesion to bond it to the surface. Any items that are subject to heavy wear and tear should be protected with a layer of varnish once the paint is dry.

Oil-based paints should always be used on metal surfaces. The drying time increases with these paints and your tools must be washed with white spirit or turpentine after use.

STAMPING ESSENTIALS

1 Colored furniture wax
2 Household emulsion brush
3 Paint kettle
4 Sandpaper
5 Denatured alcohol
6 Contact adhesive
7 Assorted blocks
8 Fretsaw
9 Assorted artists' brushes
10 Cellulose decorator's sponges
11 Regular masking tape
12 Low-tack masking tape
13 Beeswax
14 Gilt powder
15 Long-bristled paintbrush
16 Steel wool
17 Universal pigments
18 Small, sharp scissors
19 Utility knife
20 Brayer
21 Carpenter's square
22 Sketch pad
23 Foam rubber sheet
24 Scalpel

SURFACES FOR STAMPING

Almost any kind of surface can accept a stamp, provided that you use the correct paint for that particular surface. Always refer to the manufacturer's instructions before you begin. Use fabric paints on textiles, ceramic colors for tiles, and so on. The most commonly stamped surfaces are, of course, walls and furniture. Both finished and unfinished furniture are appropriate for stamping once they've been suitably prepared for painting. But equally, so are natural cotton, linen, and silk fabrics, and ceramic and glass surfaces are also appropriate for stamping, although this is not so generally realized.

USED FURNITURE

Scour local thrift shops, second-hand stores, yard sales, auctions, and flea markets for great sources of used furniture. A quick glance will soon determine whether or not the furniture is in good condition. Turn it over and look underneath, if possible, and don't touch anything with visible signs of woodworm – almost anything else can be repaired, depending on how much renovating you want to do.

There are some great bargains to be had in thrift shops. Seek out the lesser-known outlets that are away from the main street, or visit street markets for the best deals and don't be afraid to haggle.

Undoubtedly, the best pieces are those made from solid wood, as opposed to flimsy veneer or ply, and it is these pieces that will take readily to a paint finish. The pieces that I would generally stay clear of are those with heavily laminated or varnished surfaces. Modern black, lacquered furniture, which often turns up as junk and, in my estimation, rightly so, should be left alone. I also tend to steer clear of veneered items. Generally, these are discarded because their veneer is blistered – a problem that can be quite difficult to rectify once it has occurred. So, unless the piece is very attractive, I would also tend to avoid this type of purchase.

USED FURNITURE

Utility furniture, such as this wonderful old armchair, is perfect for renovation. Tables, like the glass-topped one and the beautiful table with elegant barley-twist legs shown here, are great finds, as are the sturdy wooden kitchen chairs that were picked up at a local auction for practically nothing at all. The simply styled cabinets with flat-fronted doors have perfect surfaces to work on and transform with a whole range of decorative effects.

BLANK FURNITURE

Unfinished furniture is a type of MDF-built furniture designed particularly for the home decorator. The furniture is often distributed through mail-order companies who often advertise in the back pages of home-improvement magazines. Tables, small cabinets, trays, plant holders, magazine and letter racks, candlesticks, and screens are all distributed in this way.

UNFINISHED FURNITURE

Some MDF (medium-density fiberboard) furniture is available through mail order and often arrives as a flat pack of components that require simple assembling, generally with nothing more complicated than an Allen wrench, which is usually provided as part of the pack. Other items arrive completely assembled and require only a quick wipe with a cloth before painting. You will pay a little more for these finished items, but as the furniture is still in its raw state, it will afford a considerable saving on finished, painted pieces.

I would recommend applying a thin layer of water-based, white acrylic primer prior to the base coat, as this provides subsequent paint layers with a good surface for bonding onto as well as protection between the base coat and the MDF.

Blank MDF is ideal for painting: its smooth surface is wonderful for almost every paint finish, and the paint goes on easily and effortlessly. In most cases, I use water-based latex paint for painting both used and MDF furniture. If the item is likely to receive a great deal of heavy wear and tear, then the surface is protected with either furniture wax or layers of acrylic varnish. Use ordinary matte latex colors as these have a less slippery finish than the vinyl ranges. The matte surface of the paint is then perfect for stamping, and the block has less of a tendency to slide on this surface.

Water-based paints are quite strong and durable enough for most furniture painting and they are, without doubt, the easiest colors to use. Paintbrushes are easily washed in water, as are skin, clothes, and carpet splashes, should accidents occur. However, their biggest advantage is that they dry faster than other paints. Entire projects can often be finished in the same day.

BROKEN-COLOR WORK

Occasionally I will use a scumbling glaze to produce a broken-color effect over a solid base coat. Once again, although available in oil- and water-based forms, I tend to work with the water-based equivalent. The glaze appears to be a rather milky-white color in its container but once dry, it will be transparent.

VARNISHES

For a more durable and protective finish, apply at least two layers of acrylic varnish over the painted and stamped surface. For best results, allow the first layer to dry completely, then rub this surface lightly with fine-grade sandpaper. Wipe clean and then apply the next coat.

Acrylic varnish can be purchased through most home-improvement and paint stores. It has an opaque, milky-white look but, once again, like scumbling glaze, it will dry to a completely transparent finish. This varnish is really tough and hard wearing: it will not yellow with age and will dry more quickly.

STAMPING FABRICS

When you think of stamping, almost always the idea of decorating walls and furniture comes up. However, with the right paints it is easy to print your own fabrics.

Most art and crafts stores now supply a wide range of fabric colors in small jars. These paints are thick and viscous and shouldn't be confused with the watery silk colors that are used to apply color to silk. The colors can be mixed together successfully for softer tones. I tend to purchase the primary colors, plus a white and black, and mix my own shades.

Use these paints in the same way as you would ordinary latex colors for stamping onto furniture. Pour a little color onto a sheet of glass or a flat plate and brush this outward in a thin layer. Press the stamp into the color and check to see if the paint has transferred onto the printing surface. If it hasn't, then repeat this procedure until the stamp is loaded correctly, then transfer the color to your fabric. You will find it easier to stamp by working on a flat surface. But you must first protect the surface because the paint will pass through the fabric layer. Use masking tape to secure a plastic sheet over the table, then spread sheets of newspaper over this. Next, lay the fabric over the newspaper and tape it into position. Once this area of fabric has been printed, remove the tape and lift the fabric off the tabletop. Replace the newspaper with clean sheets, then tape the next section of fabric in position. Continue until all the required fabric is stamped. For small pieces of fabric, repeat this process on a smaller scale.

Natural fabrics are best for stamping. Cotton, linen, and canvas fabrics all work well and not only in solid colors. Stronger fabric paints will stamp successfully over a checked gingham or ticking, particularly if a little white is mixed with the base color to make the color more opaque.

Checked fabrics can also be useful for positioning the stamp accurately. For the stamped fabric shades in the Nursery section of this book (*see page 110*), a small heart motif was printed in alternate squares. One square equaled the size of the printing block, which meant the heart was printed in exactly the same position each time. When printing on plain fabrics, care must be taken to accurately measure the position of each stamp in order to build up a regular design pattern.

Velvets can also be stamped in the same way, but because of the nap of the cloth, the stamped design will have the appearance of being slightly raised.

STAMPING FABRICS

A selection of plain and patterned fabrics can all be successfully stamped. Voile or cheesecloth, once stamped, can be made up into semitransparent shades, which allow light to filter softly into a room yet still maintain privacy. Strong, washable cottons are perfect for most soft furnishings. The fabric colors are permanently set by using a hot iron.

GLASS AND CERAMIC SURFACES

Frosted or plain, glass storage bottles have perfect surfaces on which to stamp. Look for those containers with perfectly flat sides, if possible – these square-sided bottles are ideal. Ceramic surfaces should be plain, such as these creamy colored plates, bowls, and pitcher. Once dry, the special paints available for ceramic and glass are washable, but they will not withstand heavy wear and tear in a dishwasher. A simple wipe with a soapy cloth should suffice.

GLASS AND CERAMICS

GLASS PAINTS

These colors appear to be very dark in their containers, but this is because they are transparent and do not contain any white or opaque pigments. The colors are strong, rather like those seen in traditional stained glass. For stamping purposes, I would recommend adding a little bit of white glass paint to the transparent color to impart an opaque quality. The colors are easily mixed together and you may wish to save small, screw-topped glass jars to contain and store colors. The particular solvent used for the glass colors is alcohol-based. For this, I would use denatured alcohol, which is usually sold as a bright purple liquid. Use the solvent sparingly as the colors are already quite thin. To clean paintbrushes, first wash them out in the solvent, then finish off in warm, soapy water.

CERAMIC PAINTS

The ceramic colors that are used for stamping are now available in all good art and crafts supply stores. Generally, the range of colors should be fairly wide, but it is worth remembering that, as with fabric and glass paints, the ceramic colors can be mixed together to produce your own specific shades.

Before stamping your design onto a glass or ceramic surface, wash the items in hot, soapy water, then wipe them with a clean, dry cloth. As an additional precaution, wipe the surface with a cloth that has been dampened with a little denatured alcohol to completely remove any traces of grease.

You will find it easier to press the stamping block onto a thin layer of paint that has been brushed out onto a sheet of glass. Press the block into the paint, lift it off, and check to see if the paint has transferred onto the foam rubber stamp. If not, then press the block into the paint once more to reload the stamp. When stamping directly on ceramics or glass, be aware that the surface may be slippery, so apply a firm, even pressure over the block once it is in place on the surface. Finally, lift the block cleanly away from the surface to reveal the stamped design.

If the stamp slips and the print isn't as clear as it should be, then it is preferable to remove the stamped design using a damp, solvent-impregnated cloth and to repeat that particular stamp again. Mistakes can often occur when stamping glass or ceramic surfaces because these surfaces are ultra-smooth and shiny, so practice on a sheet of paper first to perfect your technique. Paint colors should be allowed to dry completely before use and, as with the ceramic colors, these items need to be baked in the oven in order to fix the color firmly to the surface of the piece. Once the colors are dry, these items can be wiped clean.

PAINT FINISHES

Most painted surfaces will benefit from a soft, dappled surface or a textured finish. And most people will now be familiar with the more commonly used paint finishes that have been splashed across the pages of numerous decorating books and home-interest magazines. Over the last ten years or so, since this technique took a firm hold, we probably have all become safe now in the knowledge of how to color wash, sponge, and stencil. And nearly all of us wouldn't blink twice if asked to stipple or rag-roll. Paint effects add vitality; they bring a freshness and individuality to everything to which they are applied. Over the next few pages I'll show you some familiar paint finishes and more unusual ones too.

SPONGING

This effect is perhaps the easiest of all the paint finishes. It involves breaking up the underlying base color using thinned colors applied with a textured sponge. The sponge itself could be a small sea sponge, but it may be more cost-effective to simulate your own sponge from a decorator's cellulose sponge. Cut the rectangular sponge in half, then into quarters (if you are working on smaller projects). Pick out small pieces of sponge to build up a textured surface.

Thin sponging colors with an equal quantity of water and mix thoroughly. Dip the textured surface into the paint and dab the excess off on scrap paper. Lightly pat the painted surface with the sponge to transfer the paint. Turn the sponge to avoid building up a pattern. First sponge a darker color over the base coat, then a lighter shade and, finally, a layer of white to produce a rather sophisticated, speckled effect.

SPONGING

1 Tear small pieces from the cellulose sponge to imitate a natural sea sponge. Dip the sponge into a darker shade of the base color and then dab it gently over the whole of the painted surface.

2 When the sponged color is dry (about 30 minutes to an hour), apply a lighter shade over the first one. Turn the sponge occasionally to prevent a pattern from building up. Let dry for 30 minutes to an hour.

3 Finally, sponge a coat of thinned white latex color over the dried surface, using exactly the same procedure as before. For each color change, the sponge should be rinsed in water and squeezed dry.

COLOR RUBBING

Color rubbing is a simple technique that involves applying a transparent glaze of color over a dried base coat. The trick here is to rub the glaze over the dried base color to achieve a rather cloudy effect before the glaze dries, while simultaneously removing any excess color using either a sponge or a dry paintbrush. The finished effect is a wonderfully soft film of color that allows the underlying color to show through. When glaze is built up over a blue color, it looks like a perfect cloudy summer sky.

Color rubbing works particularly well on walls that are to be stamped and on large pieces of furniture, where a flat color would be too solid *(see page 57)*. For a soft, misty look, mix a glaze that is close in tone to the base color, one that is perhaps only a few shades paler than the base. Add a little white paint to the base-coat color and work on a test area until you are satisfied with the results.

The glaze coat is made up of one part latex color mixed together with three parts of water-based scumbling glaze. At first the glaze will appear to be rather opaque, but the milky glaze dries to a lovely transparent finish. Mix the glaze well in a paint bucket, then apply it evenly over the painted surface using a wide household paintbrush. The glaze extends the drying time of the paint by about an hour, depending on the atmospheric conditions, and helps to achieve a subtle, translucent mist of color.

Once the glaze has been applied, cut a cellulose decorator's sponge into quarters and use one piece to rub over the entire surface of the glaze while it is still wet. Rub the sponge smoothly but firmly across the surface, moving outward in all directions, but following a circular direction. The glaze will slowly start to dry and you will then begin to see the cloudiness building up. Don't overwork the glaze or it may start to streak. Turn the sponge over as excess glaze builds up, and rinse in cool water, as required.

The final effect is achieved when the glaze is dry (allow about ten minutes for this, depending on the atmosphere) and the paint marks are indistinguishable. Then all that remains is a soft, misty color.

COLOR RUBBING

1 Paint a solid base color over your prepared ground to ensure good coverage. Two coats may be necessary for this and no primer or wood should show through. Let dry (about 30 minutes).

2 Mix up the glaze color according to the proportions mentioned above. Stir thoroughly to blend the paint into the stiff glaze. Brush a layer of this evenly over the dried base coat.

3 Rub the still-wet glaze with a piece of sponge. Work it in a circular scrubbing movement to build up a cloudy effect. Let dry. As the paint layer is thin, it should be dry within ten minutes or so.

COLOR WASHING

This technique is similar to the color rubbing paint finish *(see page 21)*, although in this case the broad brush strokes left by the paintbrush are part of the overall look. The effect is rather rustic in quality and can often be seen on country-style furniture and walls. No glaze is required as the top layer of color should be very thin and transparent to allow the base to show through the faint wash of color.

Darker colors work well in this way; applying thinned colors over a paler base coat is often more successful than working with a paler wash over a darker ground. Usually, only a single layer of color is applied over the base color and, depending on the effect you require, the thinned layer of paint can be diluted in a ratio of approximately one part paint to nine parts water. A slightly more opaque wash is created by using one part paint to three parts water, but the effect is not as dramatic. Generally, the thinner the wash, the stronger the top color needs to be. Small tester pots of color can be used for the wash: a ½ pint (0.25 litre) can will probably be enough to wash an average-sized room, but do choose the most intense shade you can find. It is unlikely that you will find these stronger colors available off the shelf; they are more likely to be mixed to order on a centrifugal color mixer, so find a paint supplier who can offer this special service, as pastel shades just will not work.

You will need wide paintbrushes for slapping the thinned color over the base coat. For walls, I suggest you use a very wide 4-in (10-cm) paintbrush or even a 5-in (12.5-cm) (if you can handle it), and plenty of drop cloths (preferably the plastic variety) to protect surfaces that don't require color washing. For color-washed furniture, use a 3-in (7.5-cm) paintbrush for easier handling. Surfaces can be protected with a layer of matte acrylic varnish, if necessary, to protect the fragile surface. On walls, however, I would leave the color wash unprotected as a rustic finish should be left to age naturally.

You will find that the wash will dry quickly as you brush on diluted latex and work it into the surface.

COLOR WASHING

1 Paint a solid base coat of color over a prepared and primed surface. You may find you need to apply a second coat, once the first is dry (allow about 30 minutes), to achieve a good, even coverage.

2 Thin the required top color with water according to the effect you are seeking. For washes applied to furniture, you may prefer to work with a less diluted top color. Brush this over the dried base coat.

3 Use a dry paintbrush to spread the top color over the base coat. Brush outward in all directions to build up a patchy, uneven layer of color. The wash should be dry within approximately ten minutes.

DRAGGING

When a long bristled brush is dragged through a wet glaze, it leaves behind a subtle, vaguely striped effect, which can be very attractive on pieces of furniture as well as on some walls.

The glaze mix needs to be fairly viscous so that the dragged lines do not blur together. It is useful to set up a test patch on a scrap of old board first before embarking on the real thing. The glaze should also be fairly transparent for the clearest line definition.

Rather than mixing ordinary colored latex paint with acrylic scumbling glaze, mix a colored artist's acrylic color, as this will produce a more intense color without making the glaze too opaque. Thin the color with a little glaze first to blend it, then add this to the rest of the glaze. Brush a little glaze onto a test patch and drag the brush through this: if the glaze holds its ridged surface, then the mixture is perfect; if it is too stiff, it may need a little water. Should the color be too intense for your requirements, add a teaspoon or so of white latex color to soften it. Repeat the test procedure again until you are satisfied with the results.

When dragging on pieces of furniture, work one section at a time, either starting on the top or the legs first. Begin the dragging at a point where there is a vertical to assist your line: for example, at the edge of a tabletop or against a flat side of a drawer. Brush a layer of the glaze over the base coat and cover the entire section you are working on. Immediately begin dragging the glaze. It is important to always keep a wet edge to the glaze; never allow the area to be worked to dry out while you are working on it. Use the lightest pressure to begin the line of dragging, then increase the pressure on the bristles as you work down the line. As the line reaches the end, decrease the amount of pressure to finish. Continue in this way until you complete the work.

With walls, it may be simpler to work in a pair, with one person applying glaze as the other drags it. Glaze slows down the drying rate of water-based acrylic so it is reworkable. Oil glazes take much longer to dry.

DRAGGING

1 Apply two coats of base color over your prepared surface for a good, even coverage. For dragging on walls, it may be easier to apply paint with a roller. Let dry for two to three hours.

2 Mix together the glaze and the top color and test it on a piece of scrap, as described above, to ensure you have the correct mix and the right balance of color. Apply the glaze in strips across the surface.

3 Hold the dragging (or long-bristled) brush at the top of the glazed section. Apply light pressure at first and carefully pull the brush downward to create the dragged effect.

COMBING

This technique is similar to dragging but, rather than pulling a long-bristled brush through the still-wet glaze, a fine-toothed rubber comb is used to create the marks. The comb can be pulled straight down to create long, straight rows of glaze or it can be moved from side to side to create a wavy effect. You may also create other patterns: a cross-hatched effect or diagonal combing all produce different results. Like dragging, the underlying base color will show through the glaze so the choice of base color is just as important as the top glaze.

Special combs can be purchased inexpensively from good home-decorating stores or art suppliers. If necessary, you could even make your own comb using strong, rigid plastic or a stiff piece of cardboard.

The surface you are decorating should be perfectly smooth for combing. Any lumps or bumps will interrupt the drag of the comb and result in an uneven blip in the glaze. Mix the glaze according to the instructions given for dragging *(see page 23)*. Test the glaze out on a piece of cardboard first and assess once dry, as it will alter slightly.

You will need to maintain a steady hand when dragging the comb downward through the wet glaze. At the start of combing, you will begin working against a door frame or in the corner of a room, where you can use the molding or wall as a straightedge for the comb. However, as the combing progresses, the only guide for perfectly straight combing is the previously combed marks. Drop a plumb line to help the lines stay vertical, and support your combing hand at the elbow with your other hand.

If you wish, an oil-based glaze may be used instead of the faster-drying water-based glaze. Mix this in exactly the same way as for the acrylic scumbling glaze *(see page 17)*, but tint the glaze with artist's oil colors rather than acrylics or latex paints. The oil glaze results in a slightly more hard-wearing surface than the acrylic glazes.

You will notice that, as you end each line, the glaze will have built up around the teeth of the comb. Wipe the excess off with a clean, cotton rag before starting another line.

COMBING

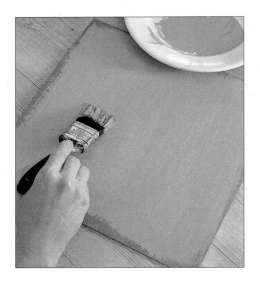

1 Paint your prepared piece of furniture with the base color. You will need to brush on two good coats for the best coverage. For an oil-based glaze, use an eggshell paint. Allow four to five hours for drying.

2 Mix up a glaze coat by tinting an oil glaze with artist's oil colors or tinting a latex glaze with acrylics. Test the effect on a scrap of board first before committing to the real thing.

3 While the glaze is still wet, pull the teeth of the comb downward through the glaze, following a wavy or straight line. Clean the comb and repeat. Let dry overnight (it will be touch-dry in two to three hours).

ANTIQUING

This technique gives the painted surface an aged look. It has the appearance of years of wear and tear on a surface, which can look particularly charming in a rustic kind of way *(see page 51)*.

WAX DISTRESSING

There are several ways of achieving the distressed look, and the technique described here is perhaps one of the simplest of all, as it uses just paint, sandpaper, and a crucial layer of candle wax.

The choice of latex colors is very important. Two colors are customarily used: one for the base coat and the other for the top coat. When the top coat is rubbed back, the first color is exposed, so the two colors must work well together to produce the desired effect. Colors that are closely related in tone will create a more subtle and harmonious effect, whereas colors that are farther apart in the color spectrum will be more vibrant. Dark green over terracotta red, for instance, would contrast dramatically, whereas creamy yellow over pale green would create a softer overall effect.

The simulated wear and tear should be heaviest at those places where you would naturally expect the furniture to show most use. Concentrate the block around handles and at the corners of a unit for the best effects. Only one coat of the base color is required. Rub those areas that are to receive heavy distressing with an ordinary candle.

The wax left behind on the surface of the paint will resist the top layer of paint because oil and water will not mix. In this case, the oil contained in the wax resists the water-based latex paint.

The top coat is then brushed on and allowed to dry. Some of the most heavily worked areas may not dry out totally because of the underlying wax, but this will not affect the paint finish. When most of the paint is dry, begin to wear away the paint layer using sandpaper. The top layer of paint will easily sand away without too much pressure. Concentrate on sanding those areas that need it most until you are satisfied with the general overall effect, making sure all traces of candle wax have been removed.

WAX DISTRESSING

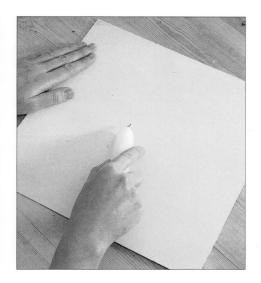

1 Paint a solid color over the prepared surface and then allow this to dry (about 30 minutes). Using a candle, scrub over the paint surface to build up a layer of resistance to the next coat of paint.

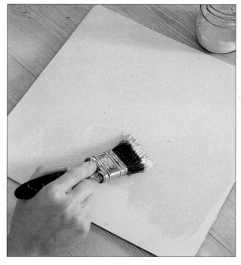

2 Next paint the second latex color over the wax to cover the base color completely. Let this color dry (allow 30 minutes to an hour, depending on atmospheric conditions).

3 Carefully rub back the paint layers with a piece of medium-grade sandpaper to reveal some of the base color underneath the surface and to produce the desired distressed and antiqued look.

SOFT-WAX DISTRESSING

This is another antiquing technique, but one that produces an effect that is softer and more blurred than that of the candle wax method *(see page 25)*. Every technique that uses wax as part of its treatment relies on the principle that oil resists water-based substances. In this way, the soft wax resists the water-based latex layer that is applied on top of it. Because the soft wax is applied by brush in a much less precise way than candle wax (which is quite literally drawn onto the paint surface), it produces a softer, distressed finish.

Both the base and top color are carefully chosen, as they each will be clearly visible in the finished effect. As with most distressed finishes, the combination of colors that you choose is the most critical aspect in determining the overall effect. Stronger colors, such as a cobalt blue worked over a cadmium yellow, will have quite a striking effect, whereas paler colors will produce a more subtle finish.

The soft wax that is used could be any one of a number of different furniture waxes. Petroleum jelly also has the same effect, although this may be a little stiffer to apply with a brush. Brush the wax onto the dried base wherever you need the base to show through. Remember that wherever the wax is placed, the top coat of paint will be resisted. Paint a generous coat of the second color over the wax, taking care not to disturb it too much as the brush is dragged over the top. Allow this to dry. Those areas of paint that are applied over the soft wax will tend to stay quite wet, but this is perfectly normal. When the paint in other areas is quite dry, you can then start to wipe away the top color. You will notice that the wax comes away too, and it is important to remove all of it from the surface. A soft cloth should remove all the wax and the damp, overlying color. Some wax will be absorbed into the surrounding matte paint, producing a silky, soft finish and forming a protective barrier. A soft wax-distressed effect is less defined than one produced with harder candle wax so that the two colors blur at the edges. I have had good results with an off-white creamy top coat over a pale oatmeal beige base.

SOFT-WAX DISTRESSING

1 Paint the base color over a prepared surface and allow this to dry (about 30 minutes to an hour). Using a soft cloth (a dry dishcloth is perfect), apply the soft wax in broad patches all over the surface.

2 When the base coat is dry, paint the second layer of latex color over the wax, taking care not to brush the wax out too much. Be generous with the paint, as lots of this will be removed later on.

3 When the second color has dried on those areas where there is no wax (about 30 minutes to an hour), wipe the surface firmly with a dry cloth. This will remove wax and paint to reveal a softly distressed effect.

TWO-COLOR ANTIQUING WITH WAX

Throughout this book, I depend largely upon a handful of paint effects. Some are built up with layers of transparent washes of paint, such as color washing; others are aided by adding transparent acrylic scumbling glaze to create softer layers of color; and some are formed simply by distressing one color to reveal an underlying one. A finish referred to as "antiquing" has become enormously popular at the moment and it is an effect I use frequently throughout this book.

There are a number of techniques used to produce an antique look but, more often than not, the look is produced when a dark-colored beeswax is applied over the top layer of color.

The antique effect can be administered over a surface that already has a paint effect upon it, but once the wax is applied, no other treatment can be used because the wax will resist everything other than itself. In two-color distressing, two colors are applied roughly over each other and allowed to dry. The colors painted on the surface will vary a little once the colored wax is rubbed over the top because of pigments in the wax. There are lots of variations in the color of these waxes, and so it may be a good idea to experiment on a piece of cardboard before committing yourself to the real thing.

To achieve a more distressed finish, apply wax with a pad of steel wool, literally scrubbing the wax into the surface of the paint. For a softer application that does not disturb the underlying paint, apply the wax with a soft, lint-free cotton cloth.

The wax gives the painted surface a silky-smooth finish, which will be resistant to the inevitable knocks and scrapes that will occur, and will also provide a wipe-clean surface. You will find that the colors used for this effect look particularly good if the tones are close. A favorite combination of mine is a green-toned off-white latex with a sage green latex *(see the tray on pages 52–53)*, combined with a heavy distress of wax applied with abrasive steel wool. The final result is quite subtle and restrained, rather like the finish that can be seen on painted antique Swedish furniture.

TWO-COLOR ANTIQUING WITH WAX

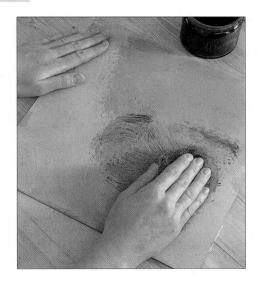

1 *Paint your first color over a prepared background. This can be roughly applied in a fairly patchy manner. Brush the paint outward so that it spreads in all directions, but keep the paint thickness fairly even.*

2 *After 30 minutes to an hour, apply the second layer of color, filling in any remaining spaces. None of the primer should be visible through the painted layers. Let dry for 30 minutes to an hour.*

3 *Load a pad of medium-grade steel wool with a tinted furniture wax. Scrub this into the paint surface to incorporate it into the surface and to remove some underlying paint. Buff with a dry cloth.*

CRACKLE GLAZE

Here is another antiquing effect that simulates years of age upon a painted surface. You may often notice that the top layer of paint on old painted walls and baseboards has started to peel and crack. This effect is easily re-created with an inexpensive crackle medium that is brushed between two coats of latex paint.

Crackle medium is available from good paint supply or art and craft stores. It is brushed on fairly thinly, so a little can go a long way. For the crackle glaze to work, you will always need to use water-based paints. Choose matte latex paints whenever possible as some vinyl paints, although water-based, can be much too slick and slippery, which makes the crackle less effective. If in doubt, prepare a small test patch first. The effect is particularly dramatic if strongly contrasting colors are used – a rich crimson red, for example, under duck-egg blue. If the colors are closer in tone, a subdued look is achieved and the effect of the crackle is then far less noticeable.

The crackle medium is applied once the base coat is completely dry (about 30 minutes to an hour). It should be applied over the surface, with the brush strokes following the same direction. Only when the varnish is totally dry should the second layer of latex be applied. Almost as soon as you start to apply the top layer you will see the crackle glaze starting to take effect. You will need to work quite quickly. It is important not to go over any parts of the freshly applied paint because the surface is rather fragile while the peeling process is taking place. Any bits that are missed can be touched up later on once the top coat has completely dried.

When dry (allow about an hour), the item can be coated in clear varnish for protection. For this, use an alcohol-based polyurethane varnish. Smaller items, such as picture and mirror frames, jewelry boxes, or night tables, look good with some or all of their surfaces treated in this way, but avoid treating larger items. On a larger cupboard or door, for example, it may be more effective to crackle glaze on only a part of the unit, such as between any paneling or around the sides, to define important details.

CRACKLE GLAZE

1 Paint a layer of the base coat over the prepared background. If you notice any lumps on the surface, sand these with sandpaper first to obtain the smoothest possible base, as they may spoil the finished effect.

2 When the paint is totally dry (allow about 30 minutes to an hour), apply a thin layer of the transparent crackle medium. Apply this carefully to some or all parts of the item to be crackled.

3 Allow the crackle medium to dry (about 30 minutes to an hour), then apply the second latex layer. Apply the wet paint in one direction only. Load the brush fully and work quickly. Let dry as before.

CRACKLE GLAZE WITH ANTIQUING WAX

Crackle glaze is used to create this finish, but rather than finishing with a layer of varnish, antiquing wax is rubbed into the peeled paint. The wax seals and protects the surface but, rather more important, it adds a depth of color that enriches the tone and lends an antiqued appearance.

Follow the same procedure as outlined for crackle glaze *(see page 28)*. The same color rules that apply to the more regular finishes also apply to this particular technique, and these are principally that colors that are clearly complementary in tone produce a more harmonious effect, whereas colors that are farther apart in the spectrum achieve more dramatic effects. Once the peeled paint is completely dry, the wax is applied. Again, for a more dramatic effect, the wax is applied with a pad of steel wool, which has the combined effect of both pushing the paint deep into the open cracks of the top layer and removing paint at the same time to further accentuate the distressed nature of the finish.

To produce a good crackle effect, it is important to brush the glaze out very thinly across the dry base coat. As the top coat reacts with the crackle glaze, the whole surface becomes quite fragile. This can be difficult to control on a vertical surface. In the past I have occasionally seen the whole top coat literally slide right off a piece of furniture. Bearing this mistake clearly in mind then, it is far easier to work on a horizontal surface. For furniture and three-dimensional objects, first work on one side of the piece. Allow this to dry (about an hour), then work on another side and so on until the piece is completed. It may be more time-consuming, but it is worth it in the long run.

If you have difficulty obtaining crackle glaze, you can make up your own medium using gum arabic. Gum arabic crystals (or liquid) are dissolved in a little boiling water to make up a sticky, viscous glaze. This is then used in the same way as the regular, commercially purchased glaze, although you may need to apply two or three layers in order to build up a good glaze coat. Test the effect on a piece of scrap paper first before beginning.

CRACKLE GLAZE WITH ANTIQUING WAX

1 Paint the prepared surface with the base color, maintaining good, even coverage. When this is completely dry (30 minutes to an hour), brush on a layer of crackle glaze and let this dry as before.

2 Apply the second layer of latex once the glaze is dry. Use a loaded brush and work quickly, as the surface cannot be reworked, applying the paint in one direction only until the glaze is covered.

3 When all the layers are dry (allow approximately an hour), rub antiquing wax into the peeled paint surface to finish the effect. Use a circular movement with the pad to push paint deeply into the cracks.

CRACKLE VARNISH

Like the peeling-paint effect of crackle glaze *(see pages 28–29)*, here is another technique that simulates an old, cracked varnished surface. In this case the technique uses two varnishes, one applied over the other, but both with different drying times. Usually the varnishes have different solvents, one oil-based and the other water-based. However, all of these two-part varnishes are different; they rely on the two-part system, but some have two types of water-based varnishes. Always check the manufacturer's instructions prior to using them.

As both varnishes react together on the painted surface, a network of tiny cracks will appear, reminiscent of the crackled varnish seen on many old paintings. The effect is much softer than that of the crackle-glaze technique. Because the cracks on this surface are so fine, it is common to rub a little burnt umber artist's oil color over the dry surface of the varnish to highlight the fine crackles. Once the base coat is dry and any surface decoration has been applied, the first part of the two-stage process is applied. The first coat of varnish is thinly brushed out over the surface. A regular household paintbrush is used to apply the varnish. If you are thinking of using this technique more often, it may be a worthwhile investment to buy special varnish brushes for this particular use as you are more able to control the amount of varnish you are using with one of these brushes.

Once the first coat is touch-dry (but still tacky when pressed), it is ready for the second stage. This second application of varnish dries much more quickly than the first and, in about half an hour, you should start to see the tiny cracks appearing. You may need to hold the object up to a light source as the cracks are often so fine. When the second layer is dry, use a soft cotton cloth to rub a small amount of brown oil color over the surface. The oil color is held in the tiny cracks, making the cracks clearly visible.

When the oil paint has dried (in four to five hours for touch-drying), the crackled surface should then be sealed with a layer of polyurethane varnish for further protection. Let dry overnight.

CRACKLE VARNISH

1 Apply a base color over the prepared surface and brush it out well. Apply two coats, if necessary. Allow the first coat to dry completely (about 30 minutes to an hour) before applying the second.

2 Thinly apply a layer of the first varnish over the dried latex. Brush the varnish outward in all directions to maintain a thin, even layer. When tacky, apply the second varnish in the same way.

3 When the varnishes are dry (in about two to three hours) and you can see a fine network of cracks over the surface, use a cotton cloth to rub artist's oil color over the surface to highlight the cracks.

LINING

This is a very simple way of adding an elegant touch to a fairly plain surface *(see also page 57)*. The lines are first drawn in by hand using chalk or a soft, colored crayon, and then they are filled in with a long-bristled artist's brush. Long-bristled lining brushes are available commercially, but these can be expensive and require practice. The longer-bristled brushes, available from artists' brush sets, will be perfectly adequate for the projects outlined in this book.

Guidelines are drawn over the prepared surface using either a long ruler or a board that will act as a long straightedge. Mark the position of the line on the surface using a ruler, then simply join these marks together with the ruler or board.

Thin a little of your chosen lining color with the appropriate solvent (oil-based color is thinned with white spirit and water-based colors need water), so that the paint is thin enough to flow easily along the marked line but opaque enough to register over the base color. You may find that it is easier to practice on a piece of scrap paper before starting on the real thing. Artists' oil or acrylic colors are the best products to use for lining as the colors can be thinned easily yet still retain their intensity.

You will find it easier to paint if your hand is supported along the edge of the surface on which you are working. While maintaining a steady hand position, one finger supported on the edge of the table or object that is being painted, place the loaded brush in position and drag your brush down the edge of the line, keeping it steady. Guide your brush slowly along the line. To retrace your steps once a brush is reloaded, pull the brush along the original line, following exactly the same path, then adopt the same hand position and increase the pressure on the brush each time you start to create a new part of the lining. Try to exert the same pressure on the brush as before, as this will determine the thickness of the line.

If you then wish to create a thicker line, do not be tempted to simply choose to use a fatter-bristled brush instead of a lining brush because you will find that this will be more difficult to control.

LINING

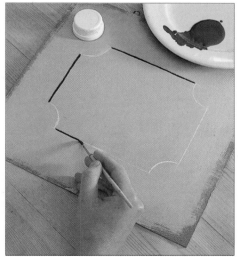

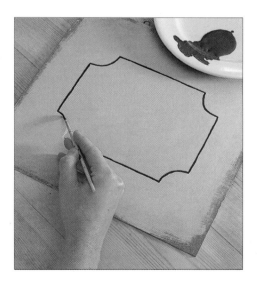

1 Mark the positions of the lining using a ruler and a piece of chalk or crayon. Join the marks together to produce the guidelines for the lining brush to follow. Draw in decorative corners, if required.

2 Use a narrow artist's brush to paint in the fine lining. The longer-bristled brushes will hold more paint than shorter-bristled ones and are easier to use. Leave gaps at the corners for the decorative details.

3 Paint in the decorative corners last. Keep a steady hand and maintain an even pressure on the brush. To achieve a neat and thicker line, paint in two parallel lines and then fill in the gap between them.

GETTING STARTED

Over the next few pages you will find all the basic know-how you need to get yourself going and (hopefully) to produce some fantastic pieces of furniture and fabulous effects around your home. The first things to consider are where to start and which stamp to use, and the projects and items stamped in this book will, I trust, give you some guidance. From trinket boxes to tables, picture frames, planters, and porcelain, I hope that we've covered just about everything you will ever need to know about decorating around your home with stamps. In the techniques pages that follow, you'll learn how to make up your own blocks and you'll find guidelines for stamping a huge range of materials. From here onwards, you'll find all the information you need to produce wonderful effects – it's just a case of starting.

STAMP DESIGNS

Once you've decided on the type of look you would like and chosen from the many designs presented at the back of this book, trace the design onto a piece of white paper. Decide whether you will need to enlarge or reduce the design. This can be done easily on most photocopiers. It is often easiest for a complete beginner to choose a smaller design at first, because the block is simpler to control.

When you have an outline that is the right size, trim away the excess. Use a small amount of spray adhesive to provide a just-tacky surface to secure the paper outline to the piece of foam. Spray outdoors if possible or fold a piece of paper around three sides of the work (sealed with masking tape) to contain the spray. If you apply too much, you'll find it difficult to peel the paper off the

MAKING A STAMP

1 Trace the motif you wish to use and transfer the design to ordinary writing paper. If you want to reduce or enlarge the pattern, use a photocopier until your design is the correct scale for your chosen project.

2 Use a small amount of spray adhesive to tack the design to the foam surface, then cut it out with a small pair of scissors. You may need to use a sharp craft knife for more intricate pieces.

3 Cut a printing block from a scrap of wood or MDF. The block must be thick enough for you to grip it at the sides with your fingertips. Smooth away any rough edges with sandpaper.

foam once the outline has been cut. Use a small pair of sharp scissors or a craft knife and cutting mat to cut all around the outline. Soft foam rubber can be cut very easily. However, care should be taken, particularly when cutting intricate parts of a design. Hold the cutting edge of the knife at a right angle to the foam and make sure you cut away from yourself.

PREPARING THE BLOCK

The more square your block, the easier printing will be. Use a carpenter's square to mark off the square perfectly and score the lines in dark pencil. The size of your block is determined by the size of the image. Use a ruler to measure both the length and width of the image accu-rately – it may be either square or rectangular. The image should fit neatly inside the block, with the edges of the design just touching but not overlapping the sides.

I tend to use thick MDF (medium-density fiberboard) for stamping blocks as it is strong, easy to cut, and does not warp. However, almost any material could be used, providing it is easy to saw and thick enough to hold between your fingertips at the sides. Look for scraps in your local home-improvement store. Cut the block using a fretsaw or power saw, if you have one. Always align the cutting edge of the saw with the marked lines. Smooth down any rough edges using fine-grade sandpaper to create a perfect block that is now ready for the foam rubber to be applied.

MAKING THE BLOCK

It is important that you transfer the drawn image of the design onto both sides of the block. Primarily, it is outlined on the front to ensure that the foam rubber pieces are perfectly aligned. You will find it is extremely useful to have the perfect mirror image of the stamp facing you on the reverse side of the block, as this will help you greatly when you are later positioning the block onto your chosen surface.

Always use contact adhesive to secure the foam pieces to the block. Do not be tempted to use any other kind of adhesive as it may either deteriorate the foam or else it may not provide a strong enough bond to hold the foam pieces in position on the block.

4 Before you stick the foam pieces down, trace the outline of the design onto both the front and back of the block. Ensure that both outlines are identically placed for accurate positioning of the block.

5 Apply contact adhesive to both the foam rubber and block to bond them. Use a small piece of cardboard to spread this evenly over the block and larger motif pieces. Allow to dry until tacky (about 30 minutes).

6 Once the contact adhesive is dry, pick up each foam section and position carefully on the block, using the outline as a guide. You can use tweezers to handle the smaller pieces. Your block is now ready for printing.

DESIGNING YOUR OWN STAMPS

It's not difficult to make your own stamps, either from your own drawings or directly from an outline that you have copied from elsewhere. Foam rubber can be cut into practically any shape you want, from fine-lined motifs to bold graphic designs. The most important tool that you will need is a sharp scalpel or craft knife. Tracing paper and a soft pencil will also be needed if you want to copy your design from another source (such as a real leaf, as featured below) or from an inspiring book or magazine.

MAKING A MOTIF

To make your own stamp motif, you will need to select your source material. In the photograph opposite, a straightforward leaf shape is drawn onto tracing paper following the outline of a real fallen leaf. The same technique may be used to draw around a single flower or a flattish shell – a scallop would be perfect. Simple shapes often work really well and, for those who may be more artistically challenged, are a great way of obtaining some quite unique original source material.

Pat the leaf with some paper towels to blot any moisture before sliding it under a sheet of tracing paper. Flatten it slightly and draw around the outside of each part. If mistakes are made, then outlines are easily erased using a pencil eraser. Use a small amount of spray mount to tack the tracing paper over the foam rubber surface (position the tracing paper over the corner of the foam sheet to minimize the amount of waste foam). Cut out the shape using a sharp craft knife on a cutting mat, following the drawn lines as carefully as possible.

Don't worry if parts of the design are separate from each other as the motif will be reassembled later. As an example, each of the separate components of the leaf opposite were cut out separately, as was the central stalk. All the pieces were then put together on the block.

MAKING A LEAF STAMP

A real leaf is blotted dry and then placed underneath a semi-transparent sheet of tracing paper on which the outline is traced using a pencil. The traced motif is then positioned over the foam rubber and *the parts cut out using a sharp craft knife. They are then assembled on a printing block and glued in position with contact adhesive. Once it is thoroughly dry, the motif is then ready for stamping.*

STAMPING WALLS

Stamping walls is easy and effective, and can be surprisingly great fun *(see pages 62–65)*. It often has an effect similar to that of a stencil, but it is much easier to do and, unlike stenciling, you don't need to follow a complicated registering procedure.

The overall finished effect is really up to you. If a richly patterned all-over design, rather like the effect of an expensive hand-blocked wallpaper, appeals to you, then the stamp is worked over a tight grid. If an open effect is more to your liking, then the same motif can be worked over the walls, but on a larger grid system. Other and equally effective alternatives include using more than one stamp design across a wall area. You will find that the possibilities for stamping are quite endless.

MAKING A GRID

The process of making a grid is much simpler than it may at first sound. For a densely patterned surface, you will need to cut a square template that is approximately 10 in (25 cm) square. Experiment with the size of the square to achieve your desired effect: basically, the smaller the size of your square, the more compact your design will be, that is, the closer the stamps will be to each other. For a much more random spacing of the motif, cut a template that is at least 18 in (45 cm) square.

Drop a plumb line from the ceiling and wait until the weighted bob lies flat against the wall (secure this to the ceiling with a thumbtack or a piece of masking tape). Hold the bob diagonally behind the plumb line so that the line crosses through the middle of both the top and bottom corners of the square. Use white chalk to mark each of the four corners of the square with a small cross. Slide the template across to line up the two sides of the template with two more chalk marks, and then mark the two remaining corners with a chalk cross. Continue working in this way, moving across the wall, until the whole area is marked with a range of small chalked crosses. Each stamp is then positioned centrally over each cross to build up a regular printed pattern.

PREPARATION

If your walls already have a freshly painted surface, you may be able to start stamping directly on them. However, for those who perhaps may have inherited rather less attractive walls, some considerable time may need to be spent on preparation before any stamping can take place.

Wipe down existing paintwork with a soft cloth and warm, soapy water and then assess the situation. If the color looks tired or is perhaps just a little too flat, then a quick and easy color wash *(see page 22)* may be all that is required to spruce it up. If you have walls that are deeply cracked and pitted, then the surface may need to be filled, sanded, and sealed first. Make these repairs and apply a base coat over the raw filler. You may need to base-coat the whole room depending on the extent of the repairs. Both of these scenarios are preferable to being faced with textured wallpaper, which is sadly ubiquitous in many homes. If your room is of average size and is covered with textured wallpaper, then I recommend that you strip away the covering, preferably with a steam stripper. These can be rented from home-improvement and equipment rental stores as well as from some supermarkets. If you are presented with a larger than average-size room covered with textured wallpaper, you will just have to grit your teeth seriously and get on with it. As a compromise, a flat color or a color-wash paint effect *(see page 22)* could be brushed over the wallpaper and then, when dry, it could be stamped. If the task is too daunting or if, perhaps more important, you suspect that the wallpaper is, in fact, holding the walls together, then it is undoubtedly preferable to live with stamped wallpaper than a pile of rubble!

PAINT

With wall finishes, the best surface on which to stamp (and to use for stamping) is matte latex paint. Avoid vinyl paints as these have a slippery and silky finish that makes your carefully positioned stamp slide off the wall once any pressure is exerted upon it. If your walls are painted with a vinyl paint on a poor surface, you have little choice but to sand down and repaint the walls. To load the stamp, pour paint into a tray or saucer and press the block into it. Coat the block evenly with a layer of paint and position it carefully on the surface. Apply an equal pressure over the block to transfer the paint. Lift it cleanly away. If any mistakes should occur, wipe these away from the wall immediately, using a cloth dampened with water; dry and repeat your stamp.

SPECIAL EFFECTS

A variety of different finishes can be achieved with the stamping block itself to add even more character to the effect. Whether you are working on smaller furniture items or larger wall areas, any of these special effects can be incorporated either onto isolated stamps or with all the stamped motifs. Small hand-painted flourishes can be quickly added to break up the regularity of a repeating stamp. A three-dimensional effect may be used along a stamped border for a chair rail. Or the printed stamp can be given a distressed look to complement a rustic effect. Exerting uneven pressure on the stamp block produces shadows on the printed motif, which works well when a more hand-painted effect is required.

STAMPING WITH UNEVEN PRESSURE

This special effect relies on the exertion of uneven pressure upon the back of the printing block. Rather than pressing evenly over the whole surface, position the block, then use the fingertips to exert pressure on the right- or left-hand side of the stamping block. This technique can be worked in a number of different ways. First, pressure may be applied to the same side of each stamp every time a motif is about to be printed. Second, the pressure may be altered randomly for each motif: first from the right and then from the left side, then from either the top or the very bottom of the printing block. Alternatively, uneven printing may be used on only a few of the stamped motifs to introduce some sort of a break in a more regular, repeating style of pattern. I have found that this effect is particularly successful when it is used on pieces of smaller furniture.

STAMPING WITH UNEVEN PRESSURE

1 Brush a little color onto a flat surface and then press your stamping block evenly into the paint. Lift the block away from the paint and make sure that the paint has transferred successfully.

2 Position the stamp on the surface, using chalk registration marks for correct alignment if necessary. Press on one side of the stamping block, taking care not to let the block slide.

3 Lift off the block to reveal the stamped image. The aim is to achieve a more strongly printed edge on the side where most pressure was exerted and a faintly printed effect on the opposite side.

DISTRESSING THE STAMP

This technique "knocks back" a neatly transferred stamp motif into its underlying base color to give an attractive aged effect. Steel wool or sandpaper is used to "scrub" the surface of the printed stamp to literally wear it away. The amount of wearing away depends on the object on which you are working. Heavily rusticated pieces benefit from a heavy-handed approach, where the resulting stamped image just ghosts through. Some stamps, on the other hand, only require a restrained amount of wear and tear to simply "knock back" the freshness of a stamp in order to help it appear slightly aged and fashionably worn.

This effect is nearly always very successful when used on either a color-washed or antiqued background *(see pages 22 and 25–30)* as this helps to accentuate the aged quality that is so desirable.

The technique works particularly well inside the panels of a cupboard door: for example, when the outside of the cabinet features an antiqued crackle-glaze paint effect *(see page 29)* or over a two-color distressed-paint effect *(see page 25)*.

The great thing about this effect is that you need never worry about achieving the perfect print every time. In fact, the more uneven the print, the better, as this quality lends a particular charm to a piece. Some stamps may be printed twice before you stop to reload.

Use emulsion paints for the stamping, if possible, as these are easier to distress. Artists' colors tend to have more of a saturated color and can stain the underlying base colors, and they are difficult to obliterate to near extinction, if that's the look that is required. The stamping effect leaves a slightly pitted texture on the surface of each stamped motif, giving the sandpaper or steel wool something to grip onto and making the prepared surface easier to distress.

For much larger surfaces, you may prefer to use a power sander to achieve faster results. Use a fine-grade sandpaper and wear away the stamped area by degrees. Check the results as you go along to control the amount of distressing. On smaller areas, however, I would recommend the hand method.

DISTRESSING THE STAMP

1 Load the block in the usual way and print the stamp motif over your prepared surface. Remove the block and repeat until the whole area to be stamped is completed. Allow to dry (about 30 minutes).

2 Use a pad of medium-grade steel wool or sandpaper to abrade the stamp. Work in a circular motion and check the amount of distressing regularly to achieve the perfect finish.

3 Repeat exactly the same procedure on all the stamps. Furniture may then be waxed or varnished for protection. Walls can be left untreated or finished with a layer of matte acrylic varnish.

STAMPING TO CREATE A SHADOW

This technique gives a stamped image a three-dimensional quality. The shadow is created whenever a paler-colored stamp is printed over a darker, ink-colored stamp. It is most important to always remember to mark the printing position of the first block so that the second stamp can be moved either slightly to the left or right of this first position. Ordinary white chalk or a soft pencil should be used as this can be easily wiped or erased when the finished stamp is dry.

The second stamping color needs to be fairly opaque so that it can cover the underlying darker color. Opaque paints invariably mean the kind that contain lots of white pigment in the paint mix. A cost-effective way of ensuring the right color, together with the right amount of opacity, would be to mix up your own shade using a matte white latex paint with artists' acrylic colors. Tint the white with acrylic color until the perfect balance is achieved. You will find that it is advisable to test the stamping colors on a piece of scrap cardboard before committing yourself to the real thing.

To mark the block, first load your stamp, using the first color, in the usual way. Position the block over the surface and lower, then press down before lifting off. Lightly mark off the four corners of the block with a piece of chalk. Lift off the block and continue in the same way, aligning the stamp with the corner marks as you go along, until the first color stamps have all been applied to the surface. Rinse the block under cool water and pat dry to remove any excess water. Then reload the stamp with the second color. Hold the block over the registration marks and move it slightly to one side, then lower and press the back of the block to transfer the paint. Lift the block off to reveal the shadow effect. Repeat as required. When all the stamps are thoroughly dry, rub off the registration marks. Try to maintain a more or less equal distance between the two stamps each time to make sure the stamps are roughly the same. Judge this by eye or move the block (say the width of a finger each time) to maintain a certain regularity of pattern.

STAMPING TO CREATE A SHADOW

1 Load the first block with a dark, inky color in the usual way, and carefully position this over the prepared surface. Press the block firmly down on the surface, exerting an even pressure on the back.

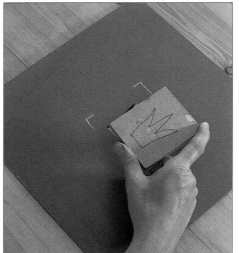

2 Lightly mark the corners of the block with white chalk or a soft pencil before carefully lifting it away from the surface. Allow the first color to dry completely (this should take approximately 30 minutes).

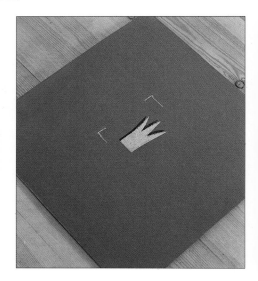

3 Rinse and dry the block, then load with the second color. Use the chalk marks to position the block. Move it slightly to one side, lower, and then press down. Lift the block away to reveal the stamp.

STAMPING WITH HAND-FINISHED DETAIL

Regardless of size, hand-painted flourishes add another dimension to a stamped surface. It need not be a grand gesture by any means: a small wispy line, dashed in to represent a stalk on a leaf, for example, will be enough. Small berries painted below a couple of holly leaves or a wavy line under a seashell can all be simply painted in as details at the end of the stamping process.

The good thing about adding a hand-painted line, spot, dash, or whatever is that nothing needs to be precise. Unlike the regular print of each stamp, the hand-painted detail can vary from one to the other: stalks on a leaf can first go in one direction and then in the other.

Generally, I would add the hand-painted details to the surface once the stamping is finished and it has thoroughly dried. This particular effect works especially well on larger areas of stamping, such as walls or larger pieces of furniture. The hand-painted irregular lines break up the graphic sharpness of a large stamped area and trick the eye into interrupting the regular pattern.

A variety of paint finishes can reinforce this visual deception. Metallic paints work well as a strong contrast between the shiny, glittery surface of the paint and the flat matte quality of the latex. Artists' acrylic paints feature some very good metallic colors, which are easy to apply and to work with, and they also have the added benefit of being completely washable in water, so any spills, drips, or splatters can be easily wiped away.

To prevent any mistakes, you may wish to draw in the proposed flourishes with chalk before committing yourself to the real thing. In this way, you can see how the final effect will look. If the look is too heavy, the chalk lines can be wiped away easily with a damp cloth, and the area can be worked on again and again until the balance is correct.

Paint the detail in alongside the chalk line, then, when the paint is dry, you can wipe away the chalk mark. Hand-painted lines can first be measured by eye, then dashed in with a confident brush stroke.

STAMPING WITH HAND-FINISHED DETAIL

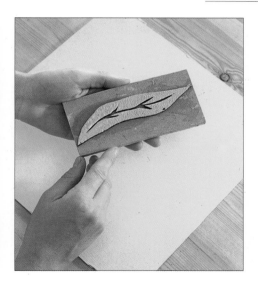  

1 Load your stamp in the usual way and position it over the surface. If you are placing the block over a fixed point, you will need to align this very carefully with the center of the stamp.

2 Press the block onto the surface, taking care not to let the block slide. Try to work on a flat, horizontal surface if possible. When stamping walls, you may find it easier to work with a partner.

3 When the printed stamp is dry, add a simple hand-painted flourish using a fine artist's brush. This could be anything from the stalk shown here to a shadow effect painted over a floral motif.

COLOR SCHEMES

Colors flavor our lives in a most powerful and evocative way. Strong reds and oranges are passionate colors, whereas cool blues and greens can be calming and restful. Every color has its own effect upon us and we tend to know what we do or do not like, particularly for our homes. Here we explore two color combinations that are currently strong and influential in the world of decorating. They are the neutrals, which are often earth colors (and many of which are derived from naturally occurring materials), and the stronger spicy palette of colors dominated by the richer shades of the color spectrum. Both color schemes are used a great deal by decorators and designers alike and, perhaps more excitingly, at the moment, stronger colors are beginning to supersede sales of white, and white with hints of color.

NEUTRALS

Inspiration comes from diverse sources: limestone tiles that have been quarried from deep earth deposits to decorative balls that are constructed from a handful of tiny beans. The neutral palette is all around us, in shells and pebbles from a child's collection, and in the simply styled fabrics and towels from a designer linens store.

The range of neutrals is vast. Certainly, it far exceeds the limited palette of cream or white, and the new neutrals greatly surpass any shade of brown. Linen, muslin, raffia, and stone are great starting points from which we can explore the whole diversity of this wonderful palette of colors. Ammonite fossils or pebbles, picked from the beach, all display their glorious colors, alongside rope, twigs, shells, and string.

LOOKING AT COLORS

Choosing the right color can be daunting, but you will find it much easier if you immerse yourself in paint charts, fabric swatches, magazines, and anything else that gives you an exciting range of styles and ideas. Literally surround yourself with paint charts and articles on a tabletop in front of you and just look. What colors appeal to you most? Perhaps you may favor the cooler shades, or maybe the warmer ones? Generally, people naturally gravitate toward their favorite colors. If selection is still tricky, start to remove those colors that you like least and then look at those that are left. Are the remaining colors all linked in some way, and do they have a common characteristic? Do not automatically despair if you already

NEUTRALS

An important consideration when dealing with a neutral color scheme is to avoid using too much of any one color. A monochromatic effect would be dull and lifeless, lacking any energy. On the other hand, a well-chosen scheme is one that uses a variety of colors and textures. Colors are layered over one another and combine well together to build up a rich effect. Natural raffia and the soft beiges and creams of pebbles all illustrate the enormous variety of neutrals that are available.

have both blue and red colors together: some blues have lots of warm magenta tones in them and thus are considered to be warm blues. Study the shades carefully and base your choice of color scheme on those colors that are still on the table in front of you.

CHOOSING A COLOR SCHEME

Select lots of objects, fabrics, or fruits (whatever you have around your home) and spread these out together in front of you, either across the floor or over a tabletop. Look at it all closely and reject anything that you may feel that you

could never live with, for whatever reason. Perhaps a certain pink reminds you of old ladies' clothes. It doesn't matter – reject it! Soon you'll have built up a collection of colors that you really do like.

Using your favorite colors in a room scheme can be very bold and sometimes daunting too. If you've carried out the selection procedure outlined here, you may be left with a deep purple as your most favorite color. Some of us could live with deeper shades, but for others, well, quite honestly, you'd have to forget it! It's all very well making a jump from cream walls to those with just a hint of color, but it takes a brave per-

son to immediately start to brush deep purple over the spare room.

Don't select a single color scheme, but look at colors in relation to others. Monochromatic schemes are just as applicable with bold colors as they are when using the neutral palette. Too much of one color can be heavy, dull, and lifeless. Think about introducing different textures, such as fabric, glass, stone, wood, or marble. Allow one color to dominate (and this will inevitably be the wall color) and balance the other colors around it. Subtle touches of one color can create a strong visual impact and accentuate the other colors around it.

When you start to decorate, the wall color will undoubtedly appear to be strong and may be overpowering, as it is unlikely that any of the furniture will be in the room while you are painting. Be brave and do not be deterred; be confident in your choice of color regardless of how different it looks on the walls, as opposed to how it looked in the can or even on the paint chart. Colors are affected by the fabrics on the furniture, the pictures you hang on the walls, and the curtains you hang at the windows. Any number of variables will alter the wall color once they are introduced into the room.

Work on a small test area before committing yourself to the whole room. Some paint companies sell paints in very small cans, which are perfect for testing. Use these colors on a scrap of board or an area of wall that isn't immediately visible (behind a sofa or door, perhaps). View the colors at different times of the day and see how the light affects them. And make sure you choose an appropriate time of day for viewing the color in accordance with when the room will actually be used.

A RICH PALETTE OF COLORS

The inspiration for these glorious colors is drawn from a number of very different sources: rich purples and plums, magentas and deep burgundies are all exquisite examples of these rich shades. Think of ripe fruit, and printed and woven fabrics from hotter climates. Vermilion, cadmium red, and alizarin crimson are all deeply evocative colors that may be successfully combined to create many interesting and varied effects around our homes.

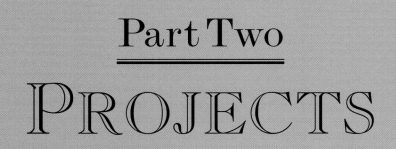

Part Two
PROJECTS

This part of the book contains projects that have been designed to enhance five rooms in a typical home – the kitchen, living room, bedroom, bathroom, and nursery. Each room has its own specific requirements – a table and chairs in the kitchen, a mirror frame in the bathroom, etc. You'll also find that every room lends itself to a set of stamps that relate to its particular style, and the detailed step-by-step sequences demonstrate how to extend the range of your stamping technique. Bold treatments are offered for a colonial-style living room, and a romantic approach is used for a bedroom. Other influences for different rooms in the house are inspired by spiraling shapes, Scandinavian furniture, and the classic fleur-de-lis motif, among many others.

The
KITCHEN

*S*oft, dappled walls in warm, sunny shades reflect the
light and create the perfect backdrop for this simple
country-style kitchen. Whether it is in the heart of the
city or the depths of the countryside, this style is appealing
to practically everyone and evokes a kind of nostalgia for
everything that is simply designed, uncomplicated, and yet
highly efficient at the same time.

The kitchen often doubles up as a place for many other
activities and is used not solely for cooking or eating. Yes, it
is a place to entertain, but it can also be used for reading the
newspaper, potting plants, sewing, writing, and painting —
any number of pastimes and pleasures in which we all
engage. It is a place that stimulates us to embark on all of
these pursuits if we wish to, or simply to sit, think, and then
wait to be inspired.

Whether you're making over secondhand furniture,
creating accessories from scratch or revamping existing
kitchen items, you should find a solution to your kitchen
problems in this chapter. And don't underestimate the use-
fulness of old junk items — both the wall cupboard and the
base units used in the projects that follow were uncovered in
dusty old junk shops and given a new lease on life.

A RUSTIC WALL CUPBOARD

MATERIALS: *Old paintbrush, paint stripper, scraper, masking tape, utility knife, soft cloths, vinegar, household paintbrush, acrylic primer, base and top coat latex paints (off-white and yellow ochre), paint bucket, crackle glaze, 3-in (7.5-cm) paintbrush, antiquing wax, tape measure, chalk or pencil, floral and leaf motif stamps (see pages 119 and 123), deep pink and dark blue latex paints, plate, acrylic varnish, screws, anchors, and replacement handles.*

Used furniture is ideal for stamping, and I was lucky enough to find this beautifully proportioned cupboard in my local thrift shop. The cupboard was heavily coated in thick brown pigments and varnish, and so it would have been a really time-consuming task to strip all the old layers away. After a little haggling, I was able to get the cupboard for a good price with that all-important delivery charge thrown in. You will need an extra pair of hands when tackling a big project like this.

As a great fan of painted furniture, I had already decided on the fate of this cupboard. The antiqued, rather rustic style of decorating certainly seems to

have captured the imaginations of many decorators at the moment, and this cupboard was about to be subjected to a makeover that would dramatically transform it from its original sorry state to a stylish piece of furniture.

Although the cupboard would have been suited to almost any room in the house, I decorated it for use in the kitchen. This room has a relaxed country style and generally has an informal feeling about it. The base colors I chose for the cupboard are soft, harmonious shades that complement each other, in contrast to the heavy, dark wood from which the cupboard was made. These colors lighten the whole look. A yellow ochre underlies an off-white latex paint, and a layer of crackle glaze *(see pages 28–29)* between the two colors splits the paint to create an instantly aged effect. The unique character of old, peeling paint is quickly achieved. Once the top color is applied over the dried glaze, the paint starts to "split" very quickly, so you must apply it as quickly as possible. With a crackle-glaze effect, the base color is visible through the top color on the exterior of the unit, so the base color was a particularly important consideration. When the effect was quite dry, I antiqued the outside of the cupboard further by rubbing colored antiquing wax all over the surface so that some wax was held in the cracks and some color penetrated the absorbent latex color. As well as imparting a wonderful patina of age to the whole unit, the wax also serves as a protective layer.

The stamping designs I used for the inside of the cupboard were very simple flower and leaf motifs that I chose for their very simplicity. I used one stamp design as a garland at the top of the cupboard and a simpler floral motif as a repeat pattern for the inside of the cupboard in bright, contrasting colors.

1 Using an old paintbrush, apply a liberal amount of paint stripper all over the exterior of the cupboard. Use a dabbing motion to apply the stripper to the surface, rather than brushing it, as this helps to make the stripping process much easier. Protect your hands and work outdoors, if at all possible.

2 When the stripper has had time to work (always refer to the manufacturer's instructions), it will start to blister away the old surface. Once this has occurred, start to strip away the old paint, varnish, and stripper with a paint scraper to reveal the bare wood underneath.

3 Once the surface is completely clear, wipe down the cupboard with a damp cloth soaked with a little vinegar to remove any remaining stripper. Let dry for a few hours or until surface-dry, then paint the whole surface inside and out with a layer of acrylic primer.

4 When the primer is dry (30 minutes to an hour), apply the first layer of latex to the exterior with a household brush. In this case, I used a yellow ochre color. When totally dry (30 minutes to one hour), apply transparent crackle glaze over the dry base coat with a suitably sized paintbrush.

5 *After approximately an hour, the glaze will be completely dry. Working a section at a time, apply the top coat over the glaze using a wide 3-in (7.5-cm) paintbrush. Try to work as quickly as possible, as the peeling effect starts to happen soon after contact with the paint.*

6 *Apply off-white latex to cover the interior of the cupboard. When the crackle effect is completely dry (about two to three hours or leave overnight), use a soft cloth to gently rub antiquing wax into the surface of the wood. The wax will have a darkening effect on the paint.*

RIGHT. *To paint the fine glazing panels for the cupboard, I taped around the edges of the glass using masking tape for quick and easy painting of the latex top coat. Once the glazing bars were dry, I removed the tape. Any stray paint marks were carefully scraped from the glass using the sharp edge of a utility knife blade, but do protect your fingers from the sharp edge if you need to use one.*

The inside of the cupboard and the shelves were sealed with a protective coat of acrylic varnish to guard against knocks and scrapes. Once this was dry (about an hour), the cupboard was hung on the wall using strong screws. Due to the heavy nature of a cupboard such as this one, we needed to use heavy-duty anchors to make sure it was completely secure and wouldn't fall down once all the china and glass were inside. For the final touch, a new handle was fixed onto one of the doors.

7 *Use a tape measure to determine the exact positioning of the first stamp and mark this position with chalk or pencil. Load the stamp in the usual way (see page 35). Print the motif on the back of the unit, following the chalked or penciled guidelines. (Here I used a deep pink color.)*

8 *Finally, load the second stamp with a contrasting color (here I used a dark blue shade) and then stamp this motif between the garlands created by the first stamp. Continue using this second stamp over the back of the unit to create a regular, repeating pattern across the cupboard.*

LEFT. *The wooden candlesticks were first given a simple, distressed-paint finish using the candle wax-resist method (see page 25). I used an off-white top color, similar to that of the wall cupboard (see page 49), over a sage green base color. A tiny leaf stamp (see page 50) was printed around the candlestick base to complement the leaves that*

were stamped inside the cupboard. Once the motifs were dry, I then applied a little antiquing wax over the surface of the candlestick to deepen the colors and also to protect the painted surface from any nicks.

The place mats were made by sewing a stamped linen panel (see page 122) over a slightly larger, woven fabric rectangle.

Always use colors intended for use on fabrics (see page 18) as these will bond to the fabric, whereas other colors will wash away when cleaned. As you stitch the linen over the base fabric, turn the raw edges under to prevent them from fraying. Press the cloth to seal the color, then tease the threads from the edges of the woven fabric to fray the sides.

ABOVE. *I used two stamps to decorate this plain china (see page 118). Always use ceramic colors (see page 19) if you intend to use the china; although these are washable, the china shouldn't be used on an everyday basis and it will not stand up to the wear and tear of a dishwasher.*

Ceramic colors are available from good art suppliers and there are two types available. One paint requires the hot temperature of an oven in order to bake the paint. Once the color is stamped on the ceramics, they are then placed in an oven at a high temperature for approximately half an

hour. The second type of ceramic color is perhaps less durable, as this is simply left to dry normally without the need for heat. I would suggest that this type of color should be used only for decorative china pieces and certainly not for those pieces that are intended to be used.

LEFT. *The tray was made from plain, undecorated* MDF *(medium-density fiberboard), which simply required a quick coat of acrylic primer before painting. Once again, to complement the rustic style of the kitchen, the colors were distressed, then antiqued with wax (see page 27). The cream-colored base coat was applied over the base and sides of the tray, both inside and out. Once dry, candle wax was rubbed vigorously over the sides. Next, a sage green top coat was painted over the wax and, when dry, the colors were distressed to give this beautiful effect.*

When the painting was completed, two different stamps (see page 118) were used to create this pattern using terra-cotta red and sage green colors and, because this tray is wider than most, I stamped two columns of the design. For a narrower tray, you may wish to stamp one central column.

Once the stamped colors were dry, I lightly rubbed colored wax over the surface of the tray to deepen the colors and also to lend an antique finish to the overall effect.

ABOVE. *This bottle rack was also made from unfinished* MDF, *which is simple to prepare. A coat of white acrylic primer is all that is needed. Rich colors were used for the distressed-paint effect – a deep Shaker blue and a terra-cotta red. The red was applied first, covering the white primer. Next, a layer of candle wax was rubbed over the surface of the dry paint and then the blue top coat was applied. Sandpaper was used to distress the two colors to achieve a satisfactory result (see page 25).*

I used two small stamps to build up the pattern on the rack – a small flower from the wall cupboard (see page 49) and the small leaf that was used around the candlestick bases (see page 50). A layer of colored wax was then rubbed over the bottle rack, using a soft cloth, to deepen the colors and protect the surface.

PRINTED CUPBOARD

MATERIALS: *An old or new cupboard, screwdriver, medium- and fine-grade sandpapers, electric sander, filler,1-in(2.5-cm) and 2-in(5-cm) paint-brushes plus an artist's brush, paint bucket, acrylic primer/sealer, sage green and gray latex paint, scumbling glaze, ruler, pencil, carpenter's square, plate, square-motif stamp (see page 123), acrylic varnish, and new handles.*

This old kitchen cupboard is one of a set of three cupboards. The chipped, red Formica tops were in a very bad state, so I wanted to replace them. I decided on a tough and hard-wearing tiled mosaic surface effect, but there are many alternatives that you can consider. If you can unscrew the entire work top away from the cupboard, then you can replace it with almost anything. A selection of natural slate or marble is a possibility, although this could be expensive. A solid-wood work top, or simply a cut piece of plywood in almost any color, is another alternative solution. Larger tiles may be difficult to cut, so if you really like the idea of a tiled work surface, hunt for tiny mosaic

tiles, which are far easier to lay. I also replaced the handles, which dramatically altered the look of the final piece.

Before you can even begin to think about transforming the cupboard surface, you must prepare it for painting. If the surface is waxed, remove as much as you can by rubbing with steel wool and turpentine. To prepare a painted surface, remove all flaking paint and abrade it with coarse, medium, and then fine sandpaper. Use a soft, dappled scumbling glaze over the base coat to cover the surface of the furniture and to create an interesting background for stamping.

I love to stamp over a broken color, rather than over a flat, uninteresting one. It really does seem to add definition to the piece of furniture and to make it appear rather more important than its humble origins. To create this type of glaze, you will need to purchase a commercially prepared scumbling glaze. This is available from well-stocked decorating stores as well as some art and craft suppliers. It is worth remembering that a little glaze goes a long way. Mix together an equal amount of glaze and paint color and stir well. Then scrub the glaze sparingly with a paintbrush over the entire painted surface to color it, creating a dappled effect. Allow this layer to dry completely before stamping over the top.

When stamping in a regular pattern, it is important to establish a grid for each stamp. Arbitrary placement of stamps will result in haphazard-looking furniture. Once I had decided that the stamped area would be centrally placed inside the cupboard doors, I marked this up with a carpenter's square, ruler, and pencil, taking my pattern into account. I didn't worry about making pencil marks over the painted surface as I knew that these would be disguised later on with a finely painted line.

1 Remove any handles and take the doors off the cupboard, if possible. Give painted or varnished furniture a good sanding with medium-grade, then fine-grade sandpapers to ensure good adhesion for the base coat of paint. For larger pieces of furniture, use an electric sander.

2 Surface holes in the wood should be filled, then one coat of acrylic primer/sealer brushed on. This will provide a base for the subsequent layers of color. Let dry thoroughly, according to the manufacturer's instructions, leaving drawers open and doors ajar if they are impossible to remove first.

3 Apply the sage green base coat evenly all over the primed surface and let dry (about 30 minutes to an hour). If the coat dries unevenly or brush marks are still visible, then apply a second coat of paint. However, make sure the first coat of paint is thoroughly dry before you begin to do this.

4 In a paint bucket, mix together a little of the gray color (this is later used for stamping) with an equal amount of scumbling glaze for the top coat. (Acrylic varnish can be used in place of scumbling glaze if necessary.) Then work this mixture unevenly over the whole surface of the cupboard.

5 When the glaze has completely dried, start to mark off the margins of the area that are to be stamped with a ruler, pencil, and carpenter's square. Measure the stamp, then mark the appropriate dimensions to determine the number of prints that are needed to cover your piece of furniture.

6 Brush a bit of the stamping color on a flat surface (an old plate is ideal) to provide an even layer of color to press your stamp into. Hold the stamp at the sides, then press firmly into the paint and lift out. Press again, if unevenly coated. Test on a scrap of paper first.

RIGHT. *This kitchen cupboard was given a sage green latex base coat, followed by a dappled coat of scumbling glaze tinted with the gray color that was later on used for stamping. Once the designs were stamped on the cupboard, a fine gray line* (see page 31) *was painted around the stamped area to distinguish the design, making the cupboard even more striking. Once dry, a coat of acrylic varnish was applied over the painted surface to protect it from damage and also to make cleaning much easier (an important consideration here).*

Old thrift-shop finds are affordable pieces of furniture that are not too precious to discourage anyone from giving stamping a shot, and the results can be just as stunning as the project featured opposite.

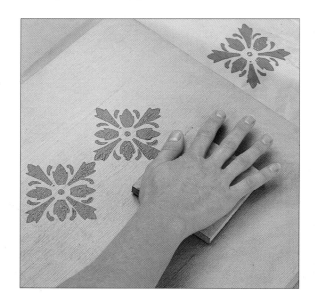

7 Position the stamp on the surface of the cupboard, using the outline marked on the back to align the motif correctly. Once the stamp is in the right position, apply firm (but direct) pressure to the back of the stamp with your palm and then hold this in place for a few seconds.

8 When the stamping has been completed, allow the surface to dry thoroughly (about an hour). For a professional finish, use an artist's brush to paint a thin line around the margins of the stamped area. When the line is dry, protect and seal with acrylic varnish.

LEFT. *This heavy pine table was made of bare, untreated wood, which meant that I was able to start immediately with my decorative paint treatment, rather than laboriously stripping away any previous coverings. Often this type of farmhouse-style furniture is simply treated with a colored wax. To remove this, you should rub the surface with a pad of steel wool soaked in paint thinner until all traces of the wax are removed.*

The stamps used for the serving tray (see pages 52–53) were put to use along the sides of this table. I had decided to use the same colors as before: a dull terra-cotta for the leaves and a grayish green for the stylized stalk. And because the sides of a table are rather narrow, I stamped the leaves first, fitting these into the space, then added the stalks in afterwards, squeezing them in between the remaining spaces. Turned details on the legs were distressed in sage green emulsion and, to finish, the base of the table was rubbed with antique wax for protection.

LEFT. *This tall bread box was simply decorated using the same two small stamps that were used for the cream-colored ceramics (see pages 51 and 118), although here I used emulsion colors on the wooden surface, whereas the ceramics were stamped with ceramic paints (see page 19).*

The background color was quick to prepare using a color-washed effect (see page 22) with colors that are very close in tone (pale and sunny yellows) to produce a soft, cloudy effect. This provided a perfect background for the silvery grays and greens of the olive sprigs. The leaves of the olive sprigs were first stamped around the box top using a variety of similar leaf colors. Olive green was mixed with black and white to vary the tone of the leaves. Squeeze a little of the basic color onto a mixing palette and, next to this, squeeze some white and black. For each stamp, mix a little black or white into the base color to alter it slightly from the previous one for a hand-finished effect. Using purplish and olive green colors, stamp the olives last of all, then finish off with a layer of acrylic varnish to seal.

The LIVING ROOM

Rich plum, ochre, and spice colors have all been combined here to create a living room with an ethnic feel. The stamp designs are strong and daring, providing a powerful decorative backdrop for a room that features furniture and accessories in striking wrought iron and heavily carved woodwork.

The bold stamp used on these walls is a far cry from the floral designs that we are likely to see in many of our living rooms. Here the stamped pattern is contained within painted panels and the overall effect has the appearance of an expensive hand-blocked wallpaper. It has a wonderfully textured finish that is particularly appealing and, rather than striving for a perfect print every time, the stamp can be uneven, occasionally missing part of the design. This accentuates the hand-crafted quality of the design, which works brilliantly in this particular room.

PLANTATION-STYLE WALL FINISH

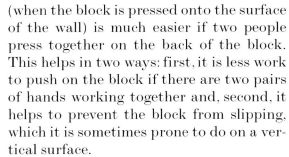

MATERIALS: *Household paintbrush, base- and top-coat latex paints in mid-toned ochre colors, paint bucket, decorator's sponge, tape measure, chalk, plumb line, masking tape, midnight blue latex paint, 1-in (2.5-cm) paintbrush, dark ochre latex paint, stamps (see pages 121 and 123), glass sheet, 3-in (7.5-cm) latex paintbrush, darker line color, and 1-in (2.5-cm) line-painting brush.*

Stamping is perfect for wall finishes as it gives the appearance of a rather expensive, hand-blocked wallpaper. The inspiration for this design came from looking at exactly this kind of wallpaper, which was used for a grand house featured in one of the magazines on interiors. The whole look has a kind of *Out of Africa* quality about it that is particularly appealing. Although it may look rather complicated, this motif is easy to cut into shape from the foam rubber and, once glued to the block, it is used in the same way as any other stamp. However, you may find the actual printing process

(when the block is pressed onto the surface of the wall) is much easier if two people press together on the back of the block. This helps in two ways: first, it is less work to push on the block if there are two pairs of hands working together and, second, it helps to prevent the block from slipping, which it is sometimes prone to do on a vertical surface.

The stamp is printed inside painted panels, which are simple to plot out on the walls using a retractable tape measure. Plan the positions of the panels first by dividing the number of panels into the length of the wall, making allowances for the gaps between each panel. Plot the resulting measurements on the wall using white chalk, then use masking tape to seal off the area to make the fine lines.

When loading a large stamp, you will find it easier to brush the paint over a glass sheet rather than a plate, as the sheet can accommodate the size more easily and also offers a more even coverage. A large plate inevitably curves upward around the rim, preventing the whole block from touching the paint. For loading the block, a regular piece of window glass is perfectly adequate, provided that you cover the sharp edges neatly with masking tape to prevent any injury.

Here a paint effect has been created for this stamp, but you may already have painted walls on which to print the stamp directly. Walls that have a solid color rather than a paint effect could also work well, although I tend to favor walls with the character of a paint finish. Simple wall washes are easy and, as the room is already prepared with drop cloths, why not spend a few more hours applying a quick wall wash to prepare a perfect background?

1 Paint the wall with a solid coat of your chosen base color using a household paintbrush. In this particular case, a mid-yellow ochre color was used. If necessary, apply a second coat of paint to achieve good, even coverage. Allow to dry for at least an hour between the two coats.

2 Pour a little of the second color into a paint bucket. Here I used a darker tone of the base color and then thinned it out with an equal quantity of water. Scrub the walls with the diluted color using a cellulose decorator's sponge to gradually build up a rather cloudy-looking effect.

3 Using a retractable tape measure and white chalk, mark up the walls to create the panels around the room. Keep checking the verticals with a plumb line as you go around the room as your walls may not be perfectly straight. Then carefully mask along the edge of the chalk lines.

4 With a 1-in (2.5-cm) paintbrush, paint between the masked areas using a strong color. (I used midnight blue.) Paint a finer line outside this panel using a different color (here I used a dark ochre latex, which I later used for stamping), but using the same technique.

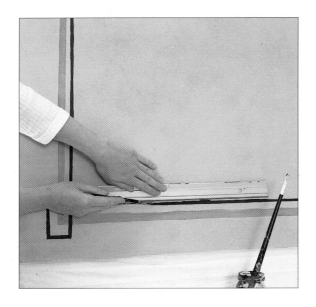

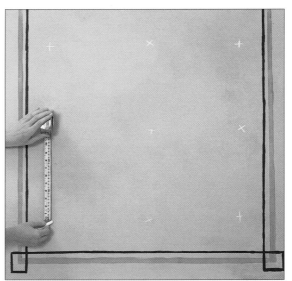

5 *You may wish to add a painted square at the corner of each of the blue-painted panels for further definition. Extend these painted lines outward to go beyond the panel and then finish them off in a neat square. Use masking tape to help you achieve much cleaner lines.*

6 *Use a retractable tape measure to perfectly plot out the positions of the stamps. Measure both the height and width of each of the panels to determine exactly the right number of stamps that are needed and then plot the center of each stamp on the wall using chalk, which can be easily removed later on.*

RIGHT. *In this room I decided to print the stamped motifs inside the painted panels, rather than as an all-over pattern. A color-washed ochre paint finish (see page 22) provides the dappled background on which the deeper ochre stamps are positioned. The larger, quite intricate motifs are interspersed with a much smaller secondary stamp, which balances the overall pattern. If too many motifs were stamped with the larger block, this would make the pattern appear overcrowded, whereas too few would seem too sparse.*

The simple, painted lines provide neat, unfussy panels which frame the stamps perfectly. A suitably exotic potted palm adds to the plantation style and evokes a certain tropical air, while a cushion in complementary prints (see page 73) and silk scarf on the sofa, as well as an intriguing pot, all add interesting details to the overall look of the room.

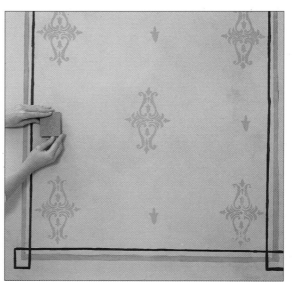

7 *Load the stamp (I used dark ochre latex here) in the usual way (see page 35) and carefully press it onto the wall. It may even be necessary for two people to press on the back of the stamp to transfer the paint evenly onto the wall, as this stamp is much larger than most.*

8 *Once the larger stamps are printed, fill in any remaining gaps with the second, smaller stamp design, again with dark ochre paint. Some parts of the two stamps may not print perfectly, but this should not detract from the overall effect of an elegantly hand-blocked paper.*

LEFT. *A full-length tablecloth and a smaller protective cloth are simply made from washable cotton fabrics. The larger cloth required two lengths of fabric, which were joined together along the long edges, with the seam across the center of the table. Dressmakers' pins were used to mark the point where the fabric just touched the floor.*

The fabric was lifted off the table and the hemline was cut, using the pins as a guide. It was then sewn, and the raw edges turned underneath in a double hem to prevent fraying. Next, the smaller, top cloth was made from just a single length of fabric, which was cut into a square. The ends were sewn as before, using a double hem to prevent the fabric from fraying.

Decorative stamps – a bold abstract pattern and a stylized leaf in fabric colors – helped to reinforce the Out of Africa *feeling. (For these templates, refer to pages 119 and 120.)*

LEFT. *This shaped planter was simply constructed from* MDF *(medium-density fiberboard). The plain, flat sides were perfect for one of the larger stamps used for the wall treatment (see page 65), and I finished off the edges with a fine hand-painted line, which neatly completed the overall look. Here the colors used were exactly the same as those I had selected for the walls, although for the base color I decided to paint only one color to produce a flat finish, rather than the color-washed effect seen on the walls.*

The planter, although originally intended to disguise ugly plant containers, is used for dried plants. But it also makes a great storage container for magazines and newspapers as well as a stylish waste bin. Seal the planter both inside and out with varnish for a wipe-clean, protected surface.

CRACKLE-VARNISHED LAMP BASE

MATERIALS:
Lampshade, acrylic white primer/sealer, paint bucket, 1-in (2.5-cm) paintbrushes, masking tape, mid-tone terra-cotta red latex, off-white top coat latex, two soft cloths, decorator's or sea sponge, tea bags, leaf pattern stamp (see page 118), plate, chalk or soft pencil, two-part crackle varnish, burnt umber oil color, and gold gilding cream.

The basic MDF (medium-density fiberboard) construction of this lamp base is perfect for a textured paint effect. When viewed from close up, the paint effect has a wonderfully crinkled, antique finish. This was created quite simply, but rather unusually, by first brushing a creamy off-white color over a reddish base color. Then, before the paint began to dry, the whole surface was splashed with water and an absorbent cloth was quickly pressed over the wet, splattered surface. When the cloth was lifted off, it took away with it some of the top color to reveal spots of the base color underneath. The paint effect works well on small items, but it would be much harder to manage on larger projects. To control the effect, work a small section at a time to avoid the top color drying out too rapidly.

After the stamp is printed on the flat parts of the lamp base, the whole thing is then crackle-varnished *(see page 30)*. The two-part varnish creates a fine network of cracks over the surface of the lamp and, although these are not clearly visible to the eye, when raw umber artist's oil color is rubbed into the surface, the crinkled surface is clearly highlighted. As a finishing touch, a little gilding cream was rubbed into the raised section around the base of the lamp using a soft cloth.

A new and pristine shade would have looked too clumsy on the antiqued base, and so a wash of strong cold tea was applied over the whole shade for an instant aged effect. Simply wipe the tea over the shade, using the sponge as if you were wiping it clean. Resoak the sponge in tea, when required. Tea imparts a soft parchment quality to fabric or paper shades to take the edge off their unfashionable newness.

When positioning the stamps around the edge of the shade, it helps to view the shade from above and to mark the positions of a clock face along the outer edge with chalk. Use each of these marks as your center line for placing the leaf stamps. Roll the stamps around the shade to transfer the paint evenly. Hold one hand inside the shade and use a little pressure here against the stamp to get a good print. Roll the block over the shade and lift off. Take care not to smudge the stamped motifs as you print the remaining patterns. The latex paint should be dry within half an hour.

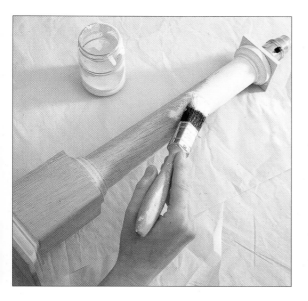

1 Prime the lamp base with white acrylic primer (one coat should be sufficient to provide even coverage), using a small brush. Use masking tape to protect the brass bulb holder and the electric cord from being painted. Let the primer dry for 30 minutes to an hour.

2 Clean the brush and then carefully apply an even coat of the base color. (I used a mid-tone, terra-cotta red latex, which was chosen to provide a strong contrast with the off-white top coat.) Again, one coat of paint should be sufficient. Let it dry for 30 minutes to an hour.

3 Apply a top coat with a clean brush, one section at a time. While wet, flick water over the surface using your fingertips. Allow this to rest on the surface for about a minute, then dab with a dry cloth. Using a decorator's or a sea sponge, smooth the top coat over the lamp base.

4 Next, gently brush a strong tea solution over the whole fabric shade to give it an antiqued look. Leave the shade in a warm place to dry thoroughly (about 30 minutes). While the shade is drying, stamp the lamp base with the leaf pattern in the terra-cotta base color.

5 *Mark the positions of the stamp around the base of the shade using either chalk or a faint pencil mark. Load the stamp (see page 18) and position it directly on the shade. Place your other hand inside the shade to make firm contact with the stamp so that pressure is evenly applied.*

6 *Once the lamp base is dry, apply the first stage of the crackle varnish (see page 30). Allow it to dry according to the manufacturer's recommendations, as these varnishes all vary slightly. Use a 1-in (2.5-cm) decorator's brush, then apply the second varnish with the same (cleaned) brush.*

7 *When the second coat of crackle varnish has dried (allow two to three hours), you may see a myriad of tiny cracks appear over the surface of the varnish. To make these cracks more visible, rub burnt umber oil color all over the surface of the varnish using a soft cloth.*

8 *Finally, to complete the aged look, rub a small amount of gold gilding cream over all of the raised parts of the lamp base to highlight the fine surface cracks. Use your fingers to apply the wax then, when this is dry, buff it with a clean cloth and then replace the shade over the base.*

RIGHT. *Here the fabric shade has been given a parchment quality by applying a simple wash of cold tea evenly and quickly over the whole surface. Once dry (after 30 minutes), the delicate leaf motifs (see page 118) are stamped around the shade. The same stamp has also been used at the lamp base and this color has been knocked back on the base to unify the whole look of the lamp.*

Crackle varnish is easy to use (see page 30) and imparts an instant patina of age to everything onto which it is applied. This lamp is no exception: the delicately crinkled surface gives a new paint finish the appearance of old age and antiquity that is so visually appealing.

BELOW. *The trinket box uses the same stamp as that featured on the walls (see pages 62–65), but in a slightly unusual way. Stamp exactly one-half of the motif at each corner of the box, then turn it around and stamp the other half on the other side of the corner. Continue in this way until all four corners of the box are printed and then stamp one whole motif on top of the box lid. The yellow ochre motifs are stamped over a deep plum base coat and finished with the crackle varnish effect (see page 30). Highlight the tiny cracks with dark antiquing wax rubbed in with a soft cloth.*

The tray has been treated in a manner similar to that of the trinket box, but this time the colors have been reversed out for a slightly different look.

RIGHT. *The pieces for each of these cushions should be stamped using fabric colors (see pages 18 and 123), then cut out. First iron the fabric and spread it out over newspaper sheets. Mark the positions of the stamp with chalk, then print in the usual way. Once the fabric paint is dry, it can be set, using a hot iron gently pressed over the wrong side of the fabric.*

Cut three pieces of fabric for each cushion – the front should be 1-in (2.5-cm) larger all around than the pad. The back is made from two pieces of fabric, both three-quarters of the size of the front to make an envelope closing. Sew piped cord between the seam for a tailored finish.

The BEDROOM

*T*he colors of this room are largely influenced by the Swedish style of decorating. Natural light filters into the room and informal details reinforce the feeling of a calm and relaxing environment. Nothing seems labored in this room: there are no fussy swags, drapes, or frilly details, and the whole feeling is refreshing and peaceful. This is a place to wind down and sleep in, or a soothing place in which to wake up and feel energized.

Bedrooms are private, intimate areas, and creating your own space away from a ringing telephone or noisy children can be immensely indulgent and uplifting. The gentle pink tones on the walls are softly color-washed with paints that are close in tone, while the stamped silvery green colors are equally soft and harmonious. Furniture is also treated with a delicate, complementary palette to reflect the surrounding colors. Nothing in this room jars or interrupts the feeling of calm. Many of the surfaces are stamped, but the overall effect never becomes overpowering.

Choose plants and cut flowers that are heavily scented, such as long-stemmed lilies, jasmine, and lilac. Delicate flowers with lots of greenery are preferable to the hothouse varieties. Be prepared to indulge yourself.

SCANDINAVIAN DRESSING TABLE

MATERIALS: *Dressing table and panels, mirror, cloth, paint bucket, white primer, 2-in (5-cm) rounded paintbrush, buff base, dark blue and dark gray top coat, old brush for mixing, chalk, off-white latex, plate, floral and chain stamps* (see pages 119 and 125), *artist's brush, masking tape, gouache, acrylic varnish, and two piano-type hinges.*

Unfinished MDF (medium-density fiberboard) furniture is perfect for this type of decoration. The smooth surface is wonderful for almost every paint finish, and paint goes on easily and effortlessly, resulting in a perfect finish every time. There are a number of suppliers who specialize in producing this type of furniture. Information can be found in the classified advertising sections of various home-improvement magazines, and we have listed some of these in the Suppliers section of this book *(see page 126)*. You may also find undecorated furniture in some home-improvement and larger home-furnishing stores.

For this particular dressing table project, I used an unusual table with pretty Queen Anne–style legs. It could be used equally well in other rooms of the house as an occasional table. However, when topped with a three-paneled screen, it makes an attractive piece of bedroom furniture.

There is a feeling of sophistication and elegance in this bedroom. The colors are largely influenced by the Scandinavian style of decoration. Cool shades and lots of reflected light make this room a place to unwind and rest. The stamped leaves featured over the walls are delicate and unobtrusive, although they are quite large in scale. They were applied randomly to create a relaxed appearance.

The pattern chosen for the side of the dressing table was inspired by a piece of Swedish furniture. It comprises a floral motif linked together with an interlocking chain pattern. The table was first given a basic paint finish and the stamped design was then applied over this. When planning the size of the stamps, the sides of the table should be taken into account. Divide the length of the longest section by the number of interlocking chain motifs required. You can then adjust the scale of the stamp design to suit. When choosing a piece of furniture for use as a dressing table, look for one that has deep sides, which are large enough to feature a strong decorative treatment like this one.

Dressing-table tops invariably become cluttered, obscuring any decoration, so I finished this one off with simple line and corner flourishes.

1 Wipe the surface of the table with a damp cloth to remove any dust. Then paint over the whole surface using white acrylic primer. Using a 2-in (5-cm) decorator's brush, brush the paint out thinly and evenly with long strokes, making sure that you reach into all the nooks and crannies.

2 When the primer is completely dry (about 30 minutes to an hour), apply the colored latex base coat. (A buff color was chosen for this project.) You may need to apply two coats (allow 30 minutes to an hour between coats) to completely cover the white primer.

3 Mix together the two parts of the top coat (dark blue and gray were used here) with one part water, and apply this roughly over the dried base coat. Use a rounded brush for this and work in a scrubbing motion. The goal is to build up a dappled paint effect with some base color showing through.

4 Use chalk to measure and mark off the positions of the larger linking motif on the side of the table. These will serve as guidelines for stamping. Pour off-white latex onto a plate and load the stamp with a small amount of paint. Press down and repeat the next pattern alongside the first.

5 Use chalk to mark the center of each link in the chained pattern and position the center of the flower stamp directly over this. Press the stamp onto the side of the table with an even but firm pressure. Lift it off and then repeat the pattern all the way along the border of the table.

6 Paint a fine narrow line around the top of the dressing table to create a neatly finished edge. If you don't have a steady hand, use masking tape to achieve a straight line. Make sure you secure the tape lightly so that it doesn't take the paint off when you go to remove it later on.

RIGHT. *The mirror is made up from a basic three-paneled screen joined together with piano hinges. I chose the same background color for the screen as that used for the base color on the table. Rather than using the same stamp as that for the table, I chose an alternative stamp (see page 118) used elsewhere in the room to avoid a too-coordinated look. The shaped mirror was cut by a glass cutter. Always remember to have the edges ground by your supplier; otherwise they could remain dangerously sharp. The mirror was fixed into place using a strong epoxy resin adhesive.*

A similar (but smaller) leaf was also stamped onto the surface of the small jewelry box. Due to the inevitable wear and tear on a box like this, the painted surface has also been treated with an application of colored furniture wax. This enriches the color of the paint layers as well as protects the surface.

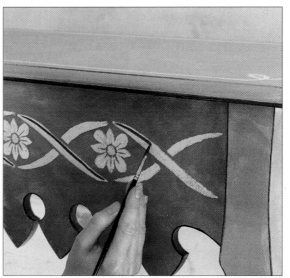

7 Rather than joining the lines in each corner, a small flourish finishes off the effect and is easy to execute. Use chalk to draw two small semicircles curving in from the painted lines, then paint over with a fine brush. You can rest your hand on the tabletop to steady it, if you need some support.

8 Use a fine artist's brush and a little gouache color (dark blue was used here), thinned with water, to add detailing to the stamped effect. Accentuate the shaped edge of the table with the same color. Once dry, add at least one coat of acrylic varnish to protect the surface and to seal the colors.

LEFT. *The soft, reflective colors of this bedroom are illustrated in a still life on a side table. Here the surfaces are all stamped, but they are in no way intrusive or gaudy. Subtle colors and simple shapes all help to create the elegance and charm that is so characteristic of this wonderfully calming style of room.*

A casual bed throw, made from natural woven linen, is patterned with the same linking stamped design used for the dressing table (see pages 119 and 125). This time, however, the stamped colors are changed to a deep blood-red and printed using fabric color (see page 18). A scalloped border transforms the casual throw into something more elegant and eye-catching. Each scallop's curve is marked off with the rim of a teacup and these are then sewn, trimmed, and turned to the right side before they are stitched onto the edge of the printed linen throw.

A hand-painted flourish, representing the stem from each leaf, extends the elegant effect over the soft, dappled bedroom walls.

LEFT. *Flat-fronted picture frames are perfect for a stamped decorative treatment as there are no fussy details or moldings to get in the way. This understated, spiraling leafy motif (see page 123) adds a certain vitality to the frame without being too ornate. Here ordinary white latex color will work perfectly well for stamping, provided that the underlying surface is abraded lightly with fine sandpaper. A layer of acrylic varnish over the dried design will ensure the stamp stays put, particularly when the dustcloth appears!*

Frame your favorite snapshots or drawings, or build up your own composite picture from cut-out black and white images pasted over scribbled on background paper. Flat-fronted frames are readily available from many stores; some are plain, natural wood frames, while others may be painted or stained. When using colored frames, make sure that the stamping color you decide to use contrasts boldly with the color of the frame.

MUSLIN SHADES

MATERIALS: *Iron, dressmaker's scissors, tape measure, muslin for front and back of shades (roughly cut to size), absorbent paper, masking tape, pencil, straight-edged ruler, stamp (see motifs, page 122), fabric paint (I mixed white with a little yellow and blue), plate, dressmaker's pins, needle and white thread, sewing machine, hook-and-loop fastener, dowel rods, handsaw, sandpaper, curtain rings, cord, and cleats (for securing).*

These Roman shades are constructed from inexpensive, ordinary cotton muslin. The double thickness of fabric allows a certain amount of privacy while still letting the natural light filter into the room. To hold the folds perfectly in shape, neat, parallel rows of doweling are required. Although these are clearly visible from the front of the shade, particularly when the sun shines, they are far from a distraction. The doweling rows add a certain interest to the flimsy fabric. As the light filters through, the stamped motifs appear to be little silhouettes against the light and the whole effect is very charming.

The construction of shades is quite straightforward. First, take an accurate measurement of the finished width and drop of the shade. It could hang either inside or outside a window recess – it's really up to you and this will depend on your particular window and its shape. Once this measurement is determined, cut the pieces of muslin accordingly. You will need to work on a large, flat surface, and the fabric should be pressed and laid out flat. Because of the flimsy nature of muslin, you should take extra care to keep the fabric as flat as possible for accurate cutting; otherwise you'll end up with crooked seams.

Cut the fabric using your own window measurements, but add 1 in (2.5 cm) all around for a good seam allowance. You will need to cut two pieces of muslin for each shade and these should be exactly the same size. Reserve one thickness of muslin and place the other over a newspaper-covered tabletop. Mark the positions of the stamp motif clearly on the surface of the muslin using a soft pencil and a ruler. The stamp is loaded in the usual way using fabric paints. I mixed a little yellow and blue fabric color into the white base to achieve a slightly off-white fabric color. Use the chalk registration marks as a guide for printing and continue stamping until the whole piece of fabric is printed.

Once the paint has dried, the shades are made according to the step-by-step instructions. To hang the shades at the windows, you will need to screw a wooden lathe across the top of the window frame. On the front edge of the lathe, staple or tack one-half of a hook-and-loop fastener. Screw brass eyes along the bottom edge of the lathe to align with the rings sewn onto the shade. The other fastener half is sewn onto the top of the shade. When pressed together, these two parts hold the shade neatly in place.

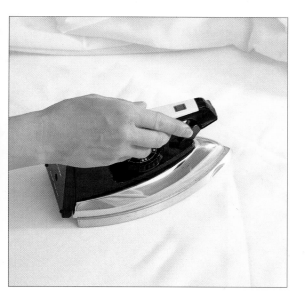

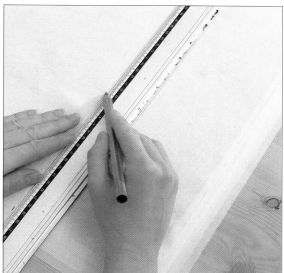

1   Press the muslin fabric with a warm iron to remove all the creases. Cut the fabric approximately to size, leaving a generous allowance all around (at least 4 in/10 cm). Lay the fabric over a tabletop protected with absorbent paper and tape this securely in place with masking tape.

2   Using a soft pencil, mark the positions for each of the stamp motifs clearly on the muslin. Use a straight-edged ruler for the most precise measuring and make sure that the first motif won't be cut in half later on once the fabric is cut out to a more accurate size.

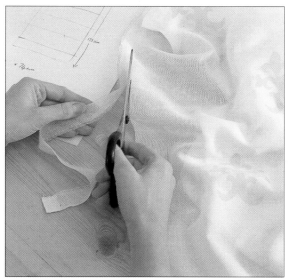

3   Load the stamp in the usual way (see page 18) and start printing. The masking tape will prevent the muslin from moving around while stamping is taking place, and the absorbent paper placed under the fabric will prevent the tabletop underneath from being damaged.

4   Allow the fabric to dry according to the paint manufacturer's instructions, then remove the masking tape and press with a warm iron. Lay the fabric over the table and cut to size. Use the measurements for your window, plus 1 in (2.5 cm) all around for a seam allowance.

5 *Pin, baste, and then machine-stitch the front and back pieces of the shade togeth-er, keeping right sides facing and the raw edges aligned. Leave the top edge open for turning through to the right side. Carefully trim the seam allowance, turn, and then press with a warm iron.*

6 *Fold the seam allowances under at the top of the shade, then machine-sew the opening to close. Then pin the second half of the hook-and-loop fastener across the top of the shade, and neatly sew the fastener in place. Trim away any remaining loose threads to neaten, and gently press.*

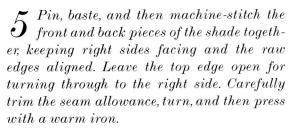

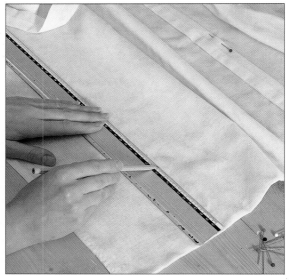

7 *Cut up strips of muslin to measure 4 in (10 cm) deep and the width of the shade, plus an allowance of 1 in (2.5 cm) for the end hems. These will make up the dowel casings. Fold the strips in half lengthwise and sew across a long and short side. Then turn the fabric through to the right side.*

8 *Lay the shade flat on your tabletop and mark a horizontal line to measure about 4 in (10 cm) from the bottom and 10 in (25 cm) from the top of the shade. Divide the remaining measurement by the required num-ber of dowels. Then, using a soft pencil, draw in the horizontal lines accordingly.*

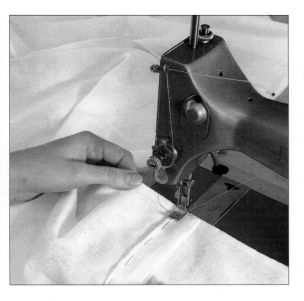

9 Pin one edge of the rod pocket over the horizontal line. Repeat this procedure for the other rod pockets, keeping the shade as flat as possible and the seams horizontal. Then machine-stitch the pocket to the shade with the stitching line positioned close to the edge of the fabric.

10 Cut the dowel rods to size with a small handsaw: these should measure the width of the shade less 1 in (2.5 cm). Sand the ends with sandpaper to remove any splinters. Insert the rod into the pocket and hand-stitch the small opening closed with just a few stitches to secure.

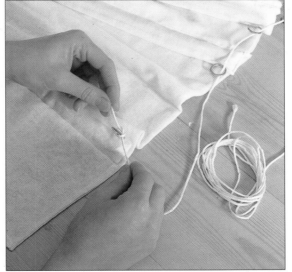

11 Carefully sew the curtain rings to the bottom edge of each fabric casing by hand, leaving intervals of 20 in (51 cm) and 1 in (2.5 cm) in from each edge. To achieve the most accurate placement, mark these points first, using a straight-edged ruler and soft pencil.

12 Thread cord through the rings, taking the cords to one side, and tie these together. Then thread through the eyes on the lathe, and tie around a cleat attached to the wall to hold. Pull into neat, crisp folds with the cords. (If you wish, a shade pull could be threaded onto the ends of the cords to neaten.)

LEFT. *Shades like these, made from diaphanous muslin that allows the light to filter through, can be left permanently closed, if necessary. They offer a solution to privacy without the need to obscure light. The shades are both practical and smart, and the stamped design is printed with fabric colors, which means they are fully machine washable (see page 18). Undo the stitching from the hand-sewn ends to remove the dowel rods prior to washing. The fabric will inevitably wrinkle during the washing process, but it can be quickly ironed back into shape afterward.*

Keep the shapes simple: use the same stamp I used here or choose your own, and print with off-white colors. Remember that fabric colors can be successfully mixed together; blend white with dark colors to produce softer and creamier shades of off-white.

LEFT. *A cream-colored fabric shade was printed using a delicate leaf motif – the same leaf stamp as that used on the mirror panels (see page 76). For curved surfaces, you will need to roll the larger stamp around the profile of the shade to transfer the paint. Use acrylic colors for the shade and blend carefully to get just the right hue.*

On the stamped side table (see page 122), a fabric drawstring bag features the simple daisy stamp that was used for the dressing table, although here it is seen without the interlocking border. Make your own bag from a combination of fabric scraps or decorate a purchased one.

A rectangular piece of fabric decorated with a scalloped edge was sewn onto a circular base for this pretty bag. Two rows of stitches provide a channel for an organza drawstring ribbon and also hold the lining fabric in place.

BELOW. *A shaped planter and tissue box are decorated with a stamp that has appeared elsewhere in the room (see page 123). Here you can see how a single stamp can be just as effective and decorative as a surface heavily patterned with stamps, as this planter clearly shows. A simple, lined edge (see page 31) provides a neat, crisp finish. The surface of both pieces is further enhanced by the* application of a delicate crackle varnish. Two-part varnish creates a fine network of cracks over the whole painted and stamped surface.

The cracks are clearly defined when a little burnt umber artist's oil color is wiped over the surface with a soft cloth. And the oil color will also subtly change the overall color, giving it a rather faintly antiqued finish.

Both of these smaller accessories can be purchased as plain, unadorned pieces made specifically for decorating purposes. You will find a number of companies that supply this type of furniture at the back of many home-decorating magazines, and their prices are often very good as they offer a mail-order service with no overheads. The tray was also an unfinished piece, but it was simply treated with a color-wash effect and small decoupage border.

RIGHT. *The wardrobe doors are patterned with a fleur-de-lis stamp (see page 122). First, the cupboard was painted with a creamy off-white base. The stamp was then printed, using acrylic colors, in a cool gray shade. Once the colors were dry, the whole wardrobe was rubbed (fairly vigorously) with a pad of steel wool and colored* antiquing wax (see page 27). The wax deepens the base color and enriches the matte paint surface, giving a soft, silky-smooth finish to the surface. This rubbing action also starts to remove some of the underlying paint and gives the surface an antique quality.

Fabric cushions are stamped with simple shapes. The spiral leaf stamp was the same as the one used for the picture frame (see page 81), and the larger base cushion features the delicate leaf stamp that was also used on the lampshade and the mirror panels (see pages 79 and 87). There are lots of stamps used here, even in this small corner of the bedroom, but at no time does the effect become too contrived or fussy.

The BATHROOM

Generously proportioned bathrooms are something of a luxury these days, but this is not a reason for compromise. This room combines natural fabrics with painted tongue-and-groove wall paneling, color-washed walls, and mosaic tiles. Even in a small bathroom there are plenty of surfaces available for decorating – a tiled splashback or a small mirror frame as well as larger items like cupboards, drapes, and laundry hampers. Wherever there's a plain surface, there's a place for a stamp.

Window coverings can be a problem for hot, steamy rooms, but these shutters are combined with strong fabric panels rather than fussy curtains for an effective solution. The fabric panels are tied onto a pole and decorated with a spiraling stamp – the same stamp as that used for the cupboard doors. Stripes on the fabric are used to determine the width of the stamp. Make sure the drapes fall short of the floor as bathroom floors are inevitably wet, soggy affairs – at least in my household – and the fabric wouldn't look as good with a dark watermark at the hem.

Don't overcrowd your bathroom with too many different stamped designs. The patterns used here all link together, usually with a spiral or circle motif, which keeps the room from becoming too contrived or fussy.

TILED SPLASHBACK

MATERIALS: *Steel tape measure, MDF or marine ply, marker pen, small saw, tile adhesive, notched trowel (if necessary), mosaic or regular tiles, tile spacers, sponge, powdered tile grout, putty knife, squeegee, cloth, stamps (see pages 120 and 124–125), black ceramic paint, saucer, denatured alcohol or ceramic paint solvent, electric power drill fitted with a masonry bit, bradawl, anchors, four strong screws, a screwdriver, and sealant.*

It's not difficult to make a tiled splashback for a small sink unit, but you will need to use MDF (medium-density fiberboard) or marine ply as both of these surfaces will not warp or twist if wet.

Use a retractable, steel tape measure to measure first the width of the area you are covering, then the height of the required splashback. Plot these measurements on your board and cut the board to size using a jigsaw or a hand-held saw, making sure your cutting lines are completely straight and the angles are perfect right angles. Mark the board with a strong marker pen before you start cutting, if necessary, and follow this line. Once

the board is cut, you will need to attach the tiles. You may use any kind of wall tiles for your splashback, but here I have chosen to use small mosaic tiles for a more interesting look. These are available from good tile suppliers, but it is worth checking the phone directory to see what companies are in your area as swimming pool suppliers will usually have the best selection.

The tiles are attached to the board with a layer of thinly spread tiling adhesive. This should be applied with a notched trowel, which will ensure that the adhesive is evenly dispersed. The tiles can then be fixed in place. If you are using mosaic tiles, these are pre-laid onto a paper-backed surface, which means that the grout spaces between each tile are exactly spaced. However, for regular tiles, you will need to use tile spacers between each tile to allow for the grout. These can be purchased easily and cheaply from your tile supplier.

When the adhesive is dry, the backing paper is soaked off (if mosaic tiles are used), and the whole surface is then grouted between the gaps. Once dry and wiped clean, the stamping can be done. Because of the nature of a splashback, the more durable the paint that is used for the stamp, the more hard-wearing the surface will be. Ceramic paints are ideal – latex or water-based paints will not stand up to any rough treatment.

Drill a hole through the splashback corners and position the splashback on the wall. Mark four holes on the wall by pushing a bradawl through the tile holes. Remove the splashback and drill holes, using an electric power drill fitted with a masonry bit. Fill these holes with anchors, then replace the splashback, lining up the holes, and screw it back into position onto the wall. Finally, an individual tile is neatly positioned over each of the screw heads for perfect concealment.

1 Cut your splashback baseboard to size, (measure the width of the area you are covering), ensuring that the sides and angles are neatly cut. Then, to make a good bed for the tiles, first scrape the baseboard all over with the edge of a small handsaw to scratch the smooth surface.

2 Next, using a notched trowel, apply the tile adhesive all over the prepared board so that the whole area is covered. Spread the adhesive out evenly over the surface using the notched tool provided with the pack of adhesive, or you could use a ⅛-in (3-mm) notched trowel.

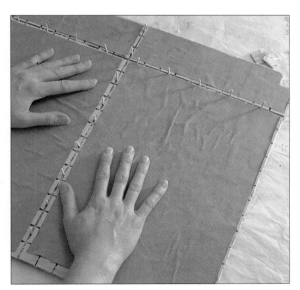

3 Press the tiles firmly to embed them into the wet adhesive surface. Mosaic tiles can be laid directly over the grout, but if you are using regular tiles, then you will need to use tile spacers. Remember to leave a gap of one tile space in each corner of the board to allow for the screws.

4 When the tile adhesive has dried out completely (refer to the manufacturer's instructions), you will need to remove the backing paper from the mosaic tiles. Wipe a damp sponge over the backing to soak it first, then wait a few minutes and peel the backing carefully away.

5 Mix about four cupfuls of powdered grout (more if you need it) with enough water to make a soft consistency that looks much like raw cake batter and spread this evenly over the entire tiled surface using an old putty knife. Roughly cover the whole surface of the board.

6 Use a rubber-bladed squeegee to press the grout deeply between the tile spaces and to remove any excess grout as you go along. Wipe the surface of the tiles with a damp cloth. As the grout begins to dry, wipe the tiles again until the whole surface of the board is completely clear.

RIGHT. *The finished tiled splashback needs to be sealed for watertightness with a line of transparent or white caulk positioned between the bottom edge of the board and the back of the ceramic sink. This sealant is available in tubes from any hardware or paint store. Occasionally, it is sold in a hard plastic tube and requires a caulking gun. However, both types are easy to use and the seal will prevent water from seeping between the sink and the tiled splashback.*

When cleaning, wipe the surface with a damp cloth, rather than scrubbing it. The ceramic color will be durable once it is dry, but it will deteriorate much more quickly if strong detergents are used.

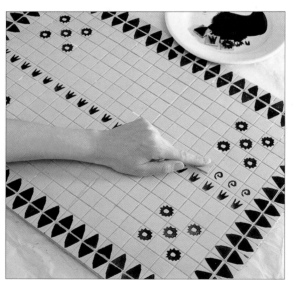

7 Make up the tiny stamps (as described on pages 32–33), *but use a single mosaic tile as the backing. (A piece of wood this size would be much too tricky to cut as the stamp is so small.) Put some ceramic paint on a saucer and apply this evenly to coat the stamp. Begin stamping the tiles.*

8 Build up the pattern according to the design used here or create your own pattern with the stamps. Use ceramic color (not the type that needs baking) to seal the colors (see page 19) and, when dry, attach the board firmly onto the wall with anchors, strong screws, and a screwdriver.

BELOW. *The small mirror frame was first sanded down, then painted with two coats of an off-white latex color. First of all, you will need to work out the number of stamps that will fit along each side of the mirror frame so that* *the stamps are printed evenly. Mark the positions of the stamps with a pencil. Print the stamps, then allow them to dry (about 30 minutes). A black line was painted between each motif, using acrylic color.* *When dry, the whole frame was rubbed with antiquing wax to deepen the colors and protect it. Any paint that is brushed onto the mirror can be scraped off with a utility knife blade.(For this motif, see page 120.)*

RIGHT. *This large bathroom cupboard was originally a kitchen cupboard, but its Shaker look was perfectly suited to the style of this bathroom. Generous storage space meant that everything that was needed in the bathroom could be* *hidden away neatly, leaving only the most decorative bits and pieces on view. The stamp featured here is the same as that used on the curtains (see page 90). Use latex paints and seal with at least two coats of acrylic varnish.* *The stamped design (see page 125) may also be repeated on the inside of the cupboard if you wish. You could even try switching the two colors around so that the inside becomes a creamy base color with a blue stamped motif.*

SHAKER LINEN HAMPER

I made this linen hamper using flexible plywood secured with metal rivets. The top and bottom were made from MDF (medium-density fiberboard) and then cut into a round shape using a jigsaw. To make the narrow band around the top of the hamper lid, I used the same flexible ply as that for the base and then stuck this around the MDF lid using strong wood adhesive. It was then panel-pinned for added security. A simple slot was cut into the center of the lid, just wide enough to push through a loop of webbing to be used as the linen hamper handle.

Almost any size of container can be used following this procedure – tall and thin, or stumpy and shallow, according to your specific requirements. It may sound crazy, but always make sure you'll be able to reach the bottom of the box when it's finished. The size of this container was about the right depth for me, but any deeper and there would have been a struggle to reach those linens at the bottom.

The small stamps are evenly spaced around the outside of the box, and some of the motifs that occur here are those used on the tiled splashback *(see pages 92–95)*. Scale the motifs up a little larger than those used before and secure the foam rubber as usual onto a wood block. I printed the motifs onto a color-distressed background *(see page 25)* and used colors that harmonized with those seen in the bathroom – predominantly the colors of the floor tiles. The off-white stamping color was strong enough to register each small stamp but not so powerful that the pattern became too important.

Other containers could be equally suitable for a linen hamper, provided the sides are smooth enough to stamp on. Wicker or rattan containers are not suitable for stamping as the open weave prevents the stamp from printing successfully.

The soft aqua blue shade used to paint this linen hamper complemented the other colors in the bathroom quite brilliantly. As only small amounts of paint are used, you will probably find that a pint can of color is sufficient for a linen hamper of this particular size.

It is always advisable to seal the paint prior to use, particularly in a bathroom, because the damp conditions may spoil the finished container. Acrylic varnish is easy to use and the layers can be applied fairly quickly (within an hour at the most), making it easy to complete the whole project within a day.

An alternative to the webbing handle would be to fix a wooden drawer knob to the top of the lid. This could then be painted and distressed in the same way as the rest of the container.

MATERIALS: *Medium-grade sandpaper, sanding block, box container of your choice, base coat colors (here I used a mid-tone blue, tinted with white for the top coat), 2-in (5-cm) paintbrush, wax candle, tailor's chalk, stamps* (see pages 120 and 124), *off-white stamp color, cloth, and clear acrylic varnish.*

1 Prepare the container (if you are making it) or choose an undecorated linen hamper. Next, prime the base coat, lid, and sides evenly and allow the paint to dry (about 30 minutes). Once the paint is thoroughly dry, rub the entire painted surface with a wax candle.

2 Next, paint a second, much darker color over the first shade of paint. You can afford to apply this layer in a rather uneven, patchy way as it will be distressed later on. Apply the second color to both the sides and lid of the container in this way to cover the whole surface.

3 When the colors are fairly dry (about 30 minutes to an hour), you may find that some types of paint may still show signs of wetness over the heavily worked, waxed areas and will not dry completely. Rub the surface of the hamper to distress it, using sandpaper and a sanding block.

4 Stamp the motifs around the linen hamper in the usual way. For even spacing and a regular pattern, you should first mark the positions of each stamp using white chalk. When dry (about 30 minutes), wipe away the chalk with a damp cloth and varnish to seal and protect the surface.

RIGHT. *The crown motif used on the Shaker linen hamper also appears along the edge of this hand towel. I cut a strip from a piece of checked fabric and stamped the motif inside the lighter-colored squares to form an edging, which I then sewed onto a towel. Alternatively, a stamped edging strip could also be sewn along the hem of a bathrobe or around a washcloth or bathmat to coordinate.*

The duckboard that you can see in both of the pictures opposite can be easily constructed using smoothly finished boards. These boards are secured at the back with two battens that were cut from the same timber and sanded down thoroughly before decorating. I used duck-egg blue for the base coat and cream latex for the spiral stamp (see page 125), then protected the surface with several coats of acrylic varnish, when dry (about 30 minutes), to make it water-resistant.

RIGHT. *The laundry bag and stool cover were made from practical cotton toweling, which can be purchased at good fabric stores; alternatively, you could use a plain white towel. Lengths of stamped fabric edging (featuring the crown stamp once more) were used to decorate both the laundry bag and the cover (as for the hand towel). The laundry bag was made using two rectangles of fabric, sewn around three sides, catching a decorative trim along the bottom. You could use tassels or fringing, or sew fabric triangles. A facing was sewn into the top of the bag and it was turned inside out. Parallel rows of stitches form a channel for the drawstring cord to pass through.*

Finally, a scalloped fabric edge was added to the sides of this stool cover before dropping it over the top of the stool for an instant transformation.

BELOW. *A yard-sale find, such as this table, can make a useful surface for bathroom bits and pieces. The collection of pebbles with holes and dried seaweed creates an interesting still life, and the creamy ceramic fruit dish makes an interesting container for soaps and sponges. The table is simply prepared and painted white. I used* white latex paint to cover the surface, and once dry (about 30 minutes to an hour), I printed a circular stamp (see page 120) around the edge of the tabletop to emphasize the pretty top, then sealed it with a coat of varnish.

To avoid the last circle squashing into the first or creating a large gap between the first and last stamp, plot the positions of the stamp before you start. Treat the top of the table as if it were a clock face: mark the main positions, then fill in as many stamps between each quarter as will fit. Print the motif using a soft gray acrylic color and edge the top with fine lining to further emphasize it. Seal and protect the colors, when dry, with varnish.

RIGHT. *These plain, unadorned containers have perfect surfaces for stamping. They can be used for almost any type of bathroom storage – cotton balls, makeup, toilet tissue, or as planters for fresh flowers.*

I used a motif similar to the one used for both the curtains and the wall cupboard (see page 125). However, the shape was made smaller and simplified somewhat. On a curved container, as in these three examples, you will need to roll the stamp over the surface to transfer the paint. Mark the positions of each motif prior to stamping. For a round container, you will find it easier to turn the pot upside down and to mark the positions of a clock face on the base. Extend the markings around the sides of the container to give you the stamping guidelines.

I used latex paint for the stamps and, once it was dry, I sealed the inside of the planter using acrylic varnish to protect the absorbent wood from dampness.

The
Nursery

Hand-painted cotton fabrics, stamped walls, and furniture are all combined here in this really bright and cheerful room. Baby pinks or powder blues are strictly banished from this altogether far more exciting and stimulating nursery. Bed linen is just as important in this room as any piece of furniture or drapery, and ordinary white cotton fabric is ideal for stamping. In addition to saving you a fortune, hand-stamped fabric looks wonderful when made up into your own crib bumpers or used to trim the edge of a fitted chair cover. A simple heart stamp elevates a more humble fabric for these Roman shades, and even a single heart-stamped panel, appliquéd onto cotton, livens up an otherwise dull cushion and chair cover.

The nursery walls were covered in a simple white-washed tongue-and-groove paneling and finished with a practical pegged rail. Above the paneling, wide magenta and white stripes were white-washed and stamped with a floral motif to provide a calm background for the more decorative elements that accessorize the room.

To complete the effect, the hearts and flowers theme is carried through and used on the storage unit. Stylized roses are stamped onto the drawer front and the backboard of the unit. The shaped leaf is also featured around the flat sides of two storage bins.

FOLK-ART CRIB BUMPER

MATERIALS: *Absorbent paper, masking tape, cotton fabric (enough to cover the bumper on both sides), long ruler, soft pencil, green fabric dye, fitch or wide, stiff-bristled artist's brush, stamps (see pages 120 and 122), purchased foam bumper or foam pieces (cut according to your crib shape), green and red fabric paints, paper (for templates), tailor's chalk, dressmaker's pins, scissors, sewing needle, sewing thread, sewing machine, ironing board, and iron.*

Depending on the type of crib, it may be necessary to have pieces of foam cut for the sides, or it may be possible to cover a prefabricated crib bumper that has already been purchased. Either way, you must check very carefully that all the relevant safety tests have been carried out on any particular product. Some research studies have linked foam mattresses and bedding with infant crib deaths, so always purchase your materials from a reputable source and never buy anything without safety labels.

The foam sides are covered in a hand-painted and stamped fabric. Stripes are first drawn, then painted horizontally and vertically across the fabric to make a checked pattern. You will find it easier to paint if you tape the fabric over a flat surface first, placing absorbent paper between the fabric and the work surface. Use a ruler and a pencil to measure and plot the positions of the stripes and join the lines together. Paint the stripes onto the fabric with powdered fabric dye that has been diluted. (Follow the manufacturer's recommendations for diluting and dyeing.) The color may bleed a little at the edges of each stripe, but control this as much as possible by painting along the edge with light movements and work quickly. Once the edges of each stripe are painted in, the inside area can be filled in.

When the stripes are dry, the two stamps can be printed onto the fabric. Once the motifs are dry, the fabric is then ironed to set the colors and cut to size. Cut the stamps from foam *(see pages 32–33)*. The heart stamp is printed onto white squares positioned between the color bands. Then, to create a gingham effect, the green stamp is printed over the intersection at each band.

Each piece is cut 1 in (2.5 cm) wider all around than the foam pieces to allow for a seam allowance and for fitting. A contrasting piping is then inset between the fabric and foam for a tailored finish. The fabric is also sewn into a tie for each corner of the bumper and inserted between the two fabric pieces. When sewing the pieces together, leave an opening for turning through and filling, then hand-sew to close the opening. Repeat the same procedure for all sides of the bumper. The pieces are then tied onto the sides of the crib.

To add another pattern and color, a contrasting cover has been made for the crib. Make the fabric ties from the same material as the bumper. For each tie, cut two pieces of fabric with tapering ends. With right sides together, sew around the sides leaving a small opening for turning. Press, then sew the opening to close. Each tie is folded in half across the center, then sewn into the sides of the bumper cover and tied around the sides of the crib. Each tie should measure approximately 12 in (30 cm) in size.

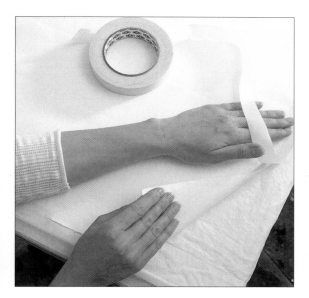

1 Place a layer of absorbent paper over a large work surface, and then smooth and tape the cotton fabric over the top. (This protective paper layer will blot up any surplus fabric dye, once it has been applied.) When using large fabric pieces, it is easier to print one section at a time.

2 Use a long straight-edged ruler to mark off exactly the vertical positions of the stripes over the entire fabric section, then draw them in with a soft pencil. Once the verticals are plotted, mark the horizontals in the same way until the whole area has been divided into a grid for painting.

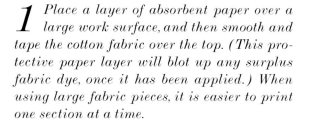

3 Next, mix up the fabric dye according to the manufacturer's instructions on the package. If the dye is warm, allow it to cool completely before using on the fabric. Use a fitch or wide, stiff-bristled artist's brush to brush on the dye, taking care not to let any of the outer edges bleed.

4 When the dye has dried completely (refer to the manufacturer's instructions), print the two different motifs over the entire fabric, using the prepared blocks and following the pattern in the photograph. Use fabric paints for the printing, blending the colors together if necessary.

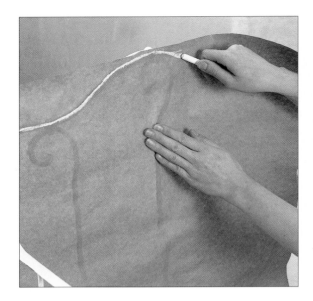

5 Make up the templates for each crib bumper section, using pattern paper, brown paper, or newspaper and following the shape of your foam pieces to mark with tailor's chalk. If your crib pieces are more regular shapes, you may not need templates – just accurate measurements for each piece.

6 Lay each of the paper templates over the fabric, pin these carefully together, and then cut out all the pieces. Make sure you add an extra 1 in (2.5 cm) all around for a seam and turning allowance, and you also will need to allow two pieces for each side of the crib bumper.

7 With right sides facing, pin the fabric pieces together with the covered piping between these layers, keeping the raw edges aligned, and fit in a finished fabric tie at each corner. Baste and then machine-sew all the pieces together. (Remember to leave an opening for turning.)

8 Turn each of the bumper pieces to the right side through the turning opening. Press, then push the corners through and fill with the pieces of foam. Add the ties, and then sew each of the openings to close and secure the bumper onto the crib. Replace the mattress and crib cover.

RIGHT. *Crib bumpers are not only decorative in a nursery, they can also help to keep your baby snug and safe. Always check with your hospital or doctor first to see whether crib bumpers are suitable for very young babies and children, as health studies relating to materials and fabrics in the nursery are being continually researched, and the information is constantly being updated.*

The plain, white inexpensive fabric used here is hand-painted and stamped to create a bold and cheerful pattern, which is then cut to shape according to the shape and size of your own crib.

Always purchase foam that is specifically designed for nursery use when making your own crib bumper. Bumpers that are purchased ready-made and only require covering with fabric should have been tested to meet the highest safety standards before being made available to the public. If in doubt, make sure you check the safety labels first before buying a bumper.

RIGHT. *This shade was made up as described in the Bedroom chapter (see pages 82–86). It is a Roman shade and is raised and lowered using cords that are gathered at the side. Here the cord is hidden behind the curtain. The checked fabric for the shade was stamped with the same simple heart motif that was used on the crib bumper. It is easier to stamp the motif more accurately if it is cut to the same size as the white square in which it is then positioned. Since the sides of the block register with the sides of the checked square, the heart motif is centered perfectly every time. Choose a thick cotton lining for this shade, as blocking out the light can often be an important consideration when you are planning a nursery.*

RIGHT. *The single heart motif was printed on a scrap of fabric. Once the edges were neatly turned under to make a square, the fabric was sewn onto a square of textured cotton fabric. This made up the front of a cushion cover (for instructions for cushions, see page 72).*

To make the chair cover, I laid a square of cotton over the chair, so that the fabric sides overlapped by about 3 in (7.5 cm). Tuck under the front corners and pin. The back was cut around the backrest, and any raw edges were turned under and hand sewn, followed by the front corners. Four long strips of fabric made the ties. Pin each tie onto the cover. Hand-sew together.

Cut a long strip from a piece of checked fabric 3 in (7.5 cm) wide and twice as long as three sides of the chair seat. Stamp the fabric and baste along the top edge. Hem the bottom, then pull the stitches to gather. Pin, then sew the ruffle onto the cover.

COUNTRY-STYLE WALL UNIT

MATERIALS: *Wall unit, two cloths, white acrylic primer, household and 2-in (5 cm) paintbrushes, base and top coat latex paints (sage green and off-white), wax candle, medium-grade sandpaper, gray acrylic color, fine, long-bristled artist's brush, stamps (see page 118), pink and green stamp paints, chalk, and antiquing wax.*

This unit was purchased as a raw MDF (medium-density fiberboard) piece of furniture in an unfinished and unprimed condition (although there was one point that was definitely in my favor – it was assembled!) The first thing that needed to be done was to wipe the entire unit using a damp cloth to remove dust particles from the cut surface. This should be done outdoors if possible as the dust particles from MDF can be very dangerous if they are inhaled.

The unit was then prepared with a coat of white acrylic primer, which was applied to all the surfaces, including

inside the drawer. Once this was dry (about 30 minutes), the paint finish was applied. A distressed color effect was applied (*see page 25*) for a softer "country" finish, which would be more in harmony with the stamped design. Apply the green base color and, when this is dry (about 30 minutes), rub a candle over the surface in all directions. The flat sides of the cupboard are perfect for this type of distressed effect. Once the wax has been applied, the unit is painted with a second coat of off-white paint. When this coat is dry (about 30 minutes) or nearly dry, as some areas of paint may not dry out fully because of the underlying wax, the paint layers can be rubbed back with sandpaper. Do this gently at first, increasing the pressure on the paper if more color needs to be rubbed off. Rub those parts of the unit that you would normally expect to receive the most wear and tear, such as around the drawer knobs or on the corners.

The flower stamps are cut from the foam using the motifs at the back of this book (*see page 118*). Cut a block for both the flower and the leaf, as these can be used alone or in conjunction with one another to produce almost any arrangement that you choose to create. Fine lining details (*see page 31*) are painted around parts of the unit: for this, use a little acrylic color, thinned with water in a saucer, and apply the paint with a long-bristled artist's paintbrush. Let the lines dry and apply the flower and leaf stamps, following the design featured here or your own pattern.

Once the stamps are printed on the surface of the unit, its newness can be toned down slightly using antiquing wax. The wax penetrates through the absorbent surface of the paint and dulls the color slightly. Rub the wax evenly over the whole surface, then buff it up to a dull sheen with a clean cloth.

1 Once the unit is wiped clean and is completely free from dust, the whole surface can then be primed with white acrylic primer using a household paintbrush. When this is dry (allow about 30 minutes), apply one layer of your chosen base-color paint. (I used an off-white shade.)

2 Next, rub an ordinary household wax candle over the entire painted surface. Move the candle outward in all directions, paying particular attention to the corners and around the drawer knobs as these will normally receive the most wear and tear and this will mimic the aging process.

3 With a 2-in (5-cm) paintbrush, apply the second top coat of paint over the base to cover the waxed surface. Let it dry for about an hour, when most of the paint should be dry, but some areas (such as the corners and around the drawer knobs) will inevitably stay wet where there is a buildup of wax.

4 Rub medium-grade sandpaper over the whole unit to wear away the top color and allow the base color to show through. The wax coat enables you to remove the top layer of paint easily without too much pressure, so do this gradually, checking the results as you go along.

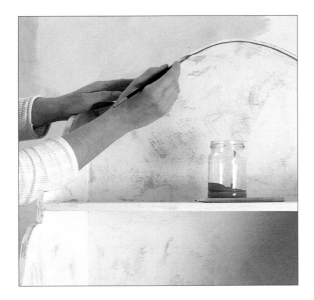

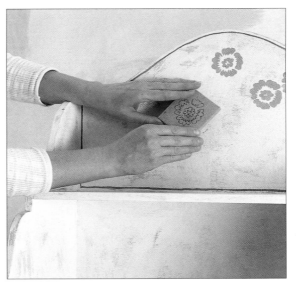

5 Using a fine artist's paintbrush and a little acrylic color (here I used a shade of soft gray), paint delicate lines around parts of the unit. The backboard of this unit is a perfect place for the lining, and I also added lining around the drawer front and sides for extra definition.

6 Load the flower-motif stamp with pink paint first and print this over parts of the unit as required. Here the backboard and the drawer front were stamped. You can assess the positions of each stamp by eye (if you feel confident to do so); alternatively mark them with tailor's chalk first.

RIGHT. *The finished cupboard is used to store all the cotton balls, creams, diapers, and other paraphernalia that are required for a small baby. As the baby grows, the unit can be used for books and toy storage and if the child throws it out when he or she becomes a teenager, well, reclaim it for your own room!*

Children's rooms offer us a great opportunity to experiment with color and patterns in a more uninhibited way perhaps than we would in our own rooms. Use these same flower stamps on a rug or around a light fixture or a door frame. You could also stamp dull storage boxes with bold colors and enjoy the effect of lots of differently patterned surfaces.

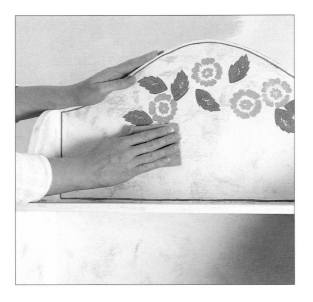

7 Load and stamp the leaf motif with green paint between the first flower stamps, taking care not to overlap any parts of the design. Visually assess the overall effect, adding another flower or leaf wherever appropriate. Again, mark off with tailor's chalk first, if you wish.

8 When all the colors are dry (allow about 30 minutes to an hour), rub a layer of antiquing wax over the surface of the cupboard. The brown tones of the wax deepen and enrich the latex paint, and the wax buffs up to a silky-smooth finish to complete the antiqued effect.

RIGHT. *Small bins are invaluable for storing tissues, cotton balls and lotions – essentially all those small items that are used regularly in a nursery that otherwise seem to become misplaced or mislaid. Each unfinished piece was given a simple color-wash treatment (see page 22) using two complementary latex colors. A single leaf stamp (see page 118), as featured on the larger bin, was used alone here, and the whole surface waxed with a colored furniture wax (see page 25). This was applied with medium-grade steel wool, which not only adds body to the colors but also distresses the paint surface, and, in this way, enhances the country-style charm of this delightful nursery.*

The larger bin was given the same basic treatment, but the larger surface area benefits from using both stamps (see page 118).

RIGHT. *The nursery walls are painted in broad pink and white stripes, allowing the plaster shades of the wall beneath to show through slightly. A stamp was applied (see page 122) in a regular pattern to achieve the hand-blocked effect.*

Padded hangers were made by wrapping a strip of batting around a wooden hanger and tucking the ends in securely. A wide strip of stamped fabric was then sewn, the raw edges tucked in, and small tucks made to ease the fabric around the curve.

For the heart-shaped pouch, a stamped fabric heart was stitched onto a coordinating fabric from which a heart shape was cut. A second heart was cut and the two pieces were then sewn together. The pouch was filled with batting and lavender heads, then finished off with a button and raffia.

STAMP DESIGNS

SUPPLIERS

UNITED STATES

All the materials needed for the projects in this book are in your local art-supply, craft-supply, fabric, or hardware store. Here are a few internet and mail-order sources to help you discover the product range available.

Al's Artistic Innovations, 549 Central Avenue, Seekonk, MA 02771 (508)761-4070. Toll-free (800)699-3193.
Web page: www.alsartinn.com
Al's Artistic Innovations is a Virtual Craft Store on the internet.

Art 2000, 24625 Del Prado, Dana Point, CA 92629, (714)488-8977
Web Page: www.art2000.com
Art 2000 is a mail-order company whose free catalog carries a large selection of paints, brushes, rollers, and more.

ASW Express, 5325 Departure Drive, North Raleigh, NC 27604
Toll Free: (800)996-6778
Web page: www.aswexpress.com
ASW Express offers art supplies for less by mail order. Catalog available.

Cheap Joe's Art Stuff, 374 Industrial Park Drive, Boone, NC 28607
Toll free: (800)835-5908
Web page: www.asrtscape.com/cheapjoe
Cheap Joe's free catalog is filled with discounted art supplies.

Craft King, PO Box 90637, Lakeland, FL 33804 (813)648-2969
Toll free: (800)769-9494
Craft King is a mail-order company that offers discounts on over 10,000 items.

Daniel Smith Catalog of Artist's Materials, 4150 First Avenue South, Seattle, WA 98124-5568 (206)223-9699
Toll free: (800)426-6740
Daniel Smith's stores carry a complete selection of art supplies. Free catalog.

Dick Blick Art Materials, PO Box 1267, Galesburg, IL 61402-1267
(319)343-6181. Toll-free: (800)447-8192
Web page: www.dickblick.com
Dick Blick's free catalog includes paints, varnishes, stains, waxes, wood blocks, sponges, and Soft-Kut® Printing Blocks.

Dharma Trading Co., PO Box 150916, San Rafael, CA 94915 (415)456-7657
Toll-free: (800)542-5227
Web Page: www.dharmatrading.com
Dharma Trading Company's Textile Supply Catalog carries art supplies. Includes untreated fabrics, brushes, paints, sponges, and Flexible Printing Plates®. Free catalog.

Hobby Lobby Creative Centers
Web Page: www.hobbylobby.com/
Hobby Lobby offers a quality selection of merchandise in their 146 stores. Visit their web page or order from their catalog.

Home Depot Stores,
Webb page: www.HomeDepot.com
Home Depot is your source for latex paints, adhesives, stains, paint thinners, brushes, foam, and much more. Catalog available.

Jerry's Catalog, PO Box 58638, Raleigh, NC 27658. (919)878-6782. Toll-free: (800)827-8478. Web Page: www.jerryscatalog.com/
Jerry's Catalog is filled with Art and Crafts supplies at discount prices. Catalog is on the internet or call for a free copy.

Michaels, Inc., the Arts & Crafts Store, PO Box 619566, Dallas-Forth Worth, TX 75261 Web Page: www.michaels.com
Michaels is the largest arts and craft retail chain. Visit their web page.

New York Central Art Supply Co., 62 Third Avenue, New York, NY 10003 (212)477-0400 Toll free: (800)950-6111.
New York Central Art Supply is one of the premier art suppliers in the country. Two catalogs available; art supplies and fine art papers.

Old America Stores, Inc., 811 North Collins Freeway, Highway 75, PO Box 370, Howe, TX 75459 Web Page: www.oldamerica.com
Old America and Crafts America Stores are a complete supply source. Order via the internet.

Pearl Paint, 308 Canal Street, New York, NY 10013. (212)431-7932.
Toll-free: (800)221-6845 Web Page: http://pearlpaint.com/pearl/ index.html/
Pearl Paint has 19 locations across the United States and an international mail-order department. Call for a catalog or visit their web page.

Sam Flax, 39 East 19th Street, New York, NY 10011 (212)620-3000.
Sam Flax has a large art-supply store in New York City and a wonderful catalog with an immense supply of art materials.

UNITED KINGDOM

* *Indicates that mail order is available.*

J.W. Bollom & Co. Ltd., 121 South Liberty Lane, Ashton Vale, Bristol BS3 2SZ.
Tel. (01179) 665151 Fax (01179) 667180
For paints.

*L. Cornelissen & Son Ltd., 105 Great Russell Street, London WC1B 3RY.
Tel. (0171) 636 1045 Fax (0171) 636 3655
For all gilding and artist's materials.

*Green & Stone of Chelsea, 259 Kings Road, London SW3 5EL.
Tel. (0171) 352 0837 Fax (0171) 351 1098
For paints and finishes, brushes, art materials, cut-outs, scumble, and varnishes.

J.D. McDougall Ltd., 4 McGrath Road, London E15 4JP.
Tel. (0181) 534 2921 Fax (0181) 519 8423
For canvas, textile fabrics, and hessian.

*John S. Oliver Ltd., 33 Pembridge Road, London W11 3HG.
Tel. (0171) 221 6466 Fax (0171) 727 5555
For their own range of paint colours, fabrics, and papers.

*London Graphic Centre, 16 Shelton Street, London WC2H 9JG.
Tel. (0171) 240 0095 Fax (0171) 831 1544
For fabric paints, graphics, and artist's and architectural materials.

*Nutshell Natural Paints, Hamlyn House, Mardle Way, Buckfastleigh, Devon TQ11 0NR.
Tel. (013646) 42892 Fax (013646) 643888
For earth and mineral pigments, varnishes, natural paints, and waxes.

*Papers & Paints Ltd., 4 Park Walk, London SW10 0AD.
Tel. (0171) 352 8626 Fax (0171) 352 1017
For specialist paints and glazes.

*Pentonville Rubber Products Ltd., 104/106 Pentonville Road, London N1 9JB.
Tel. (0171) 837 4582 Fax (0171) 278 7392
For foam rubber sheeting.

*E. Ploton (Sundries) Ltd., 273 Archway Road, London N6 5AA.
Tel. (0181) 348 0315 Fax (0181) 348 3414
For artist's and gilding materials.

*J.H. Ratcliffe & Co. (Paints) Ltd., 135a Linaker Street, Southport PR8 5DF.
Tel. (01704) 537999 Fax (01704) 544138
For scumble glazes, varnishes, tools, etc.

*Reed Harris, Riverside House, 27 Carnwath Road, London SW6 3HR.
Tel. (0171) 736 7511 Fax. (0171) 736 2988
For wall and floor finishes, and unglazed mosaic tiles.

*Russell & Chapple Ltd., 23 Monmouth Street, Covent Garden, London WC2H 9DE.
Tel. (0171) 836 7521 Fax (0171) 497 0554
For canvas, hessian, and art materials.

*Scumble Goosie, Lewiston Mill, Brinscombe, Stroud, Gloucestershire GL5 2TB.
Tel. (01453) 731305 Fax (as phone)
For a range of MDF "blanks," paints, etc.

BIBLIOGRAPHY AND FURTHER READING

Ballantine, Belinda. *The Decoupage Kit*, London, Little, Brown & Company, 1993

Ballantine, Belinda. *The Furniture Painting Kit*, London, Little, Brown & Company, 1995

Barker, Linda. *Simply Paint*, London, Collins & Brown Publishers, 1993

Barker, Linda. *Simply Fabric*, London, Collins & Brown Publishers, 1993

Barker, Linda. *Simply Paper*, London, Collins & Brown Publishers, 1994

Barker, Linda. *Simply Stencilling*, London, Collins & Brown Publishers, 1994

Barker, Linda. *Simply Colour*, London, Collins & Brown Publishers, 1994

Barker, Linda. *Simply Curtains*, London, Collins & Brown Publishers, 1995

Barker, Linda. *Making Cushions*, London, Salamander Books, 1995

Barker, Linda. *Just Junk*, Newton Abbot, David & Charles Publishers, 1997

Cavelle, Simon. *The Encyclopedia of Decorative Paint Effects*, London, Headline, 1994

Drucker, Mindy & Finkelstein, Pierre. *Recipes for Surfaces*, London, Cassell, 1992. Also pub. in USA, Running Heads Inc., 1990

Innes, Jocasta. *Paintwise*, London, Pyramid, 1991

McCloud, Kevin. *Kevin McCloud's Decorating Book*, London, Dorling Kindersley, 1990

Sloan, Annie & Gwynn, Kate. *The Complete Book of Decorative Paint Techniques*, London, Century Hutchinson, 1988

INDEX

Page numbers in *italics* refer to illustrations.

Acknowledgments

AUTHOR'S ACKNOWLEDGMENTS

With many thanks to all those at Eddison Sadd who have helped to get this book to press,
and to Lizzie Orme whose photography is truly inspirational.

EDDISON · SADD EDITIONS

Commissioning Editor   Zoë Hughes
Project Editor   Jane Donovan
Proofreader   Nikky Twyman
Indexer   Dorothy Frame

Art Director   Elaine Partington
Senior Art Editor   Sarah Howerd
Designers   Lynne Ross and
                        Shefton Somersall-Weekes
Photographer   Lizzie Orme
Line Illustrations   Anthony Duke

Production   Hazel Kirkman and
                        Charles James

PICTURE CREDITS

The photographs on page 7 are reproduced by kind permission of Arthur Sanderson & Sons Ltd.